D1306316

Polar Scientists Studying the Antarctic

Polar Scientists
Studying the Antarctic

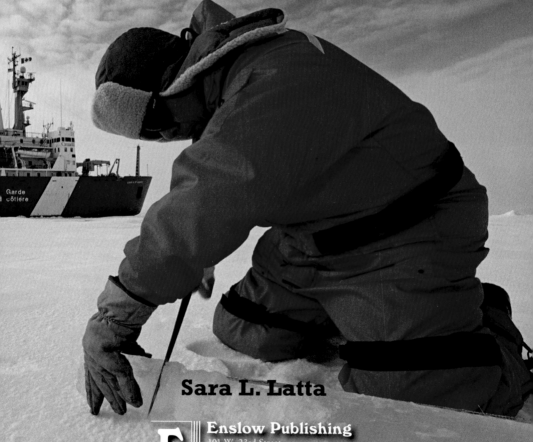

Sara L. Latta

Enslow Publishing
101 W. 23rd Street
Suite 240
New York, NY 10011
USA

enslow.com

Published in 2016 by Enslow Publishing, LLC
101 W. 23rd Street, Suite 240, New York, NY 10011

Library of Congress Cataloging-in-Publication Data
Latta, Sara L.
 Polar scientists : studying the Antarctic / Sara L. Latta.
   pages cm. — (Extreme science careers)
 Audience: 12-up.
 Audience: Grade 7 to 8.
 Includes bibliographical references and index.
 Summary: "Discusses careers in polar science, including education, training, specialties, and salaries"—Provided by publisher.
 ISBN 978-0-7660-6966-4
 1. Scientists—Polar regions—Juvenile literature. 2. Polar regions—Research—Juvenile literature. I. Title.
 G863.L37 2015
 559.89023—dc23
                        2015011326

Printed in the United States of America

To Our Readers: We have done our best to make sure all Web site addresses in this book were active and appropriate when we went to press. However, the author and the publisher have no control over and assume no liability for the material available on those Web sites or on any Web sites they may link to. Any comments or suggestions can be sent by e-mail to customerservice@enslow.com.

Portions of this book originally appeared in the book *Ice Scientist: Careers in the Frozen Antarctic*.

Contents

The ice of Antarctica contains clues to the history of the earth's climate. Researchers use what they learn here to better understand what is in store for the future.

Chapter 1

This Laboratory Is Freezing!

urrounding the South Pole, Antarctica is the coldest, driest, highest, and windiest place on the earth. A thick sheet of ice covers nearly all of the continent. All around this icy land are giant icebergs, pack ice, and rough ocean waves. Living and working in Antarctica can be a real challenge, even dangerous. Yet many scientists find themselves returning to this frozen continent year after year.

Imagine a day as a field scientist in Antarctica. You and your tent mate awaken from your sleep, cozy in your sleeping bags. The sunlight filters in through your bright yellow tent, bathing you and your companion in light as you melt snow to make breakfast on your cooking stove. Outside, it is –20°F (–29°C), so you dress warmly, layer upon layer. You begin with a layer of lightweight materials that will draw any moisture away from your body. You add a middle layer of loose-fitting clothes that trap air and body warmth. Over this goes a layer of windproof and waterproof clothing that lets any moisture from your body escape. Do not forget your head and neck warmers, insulated boots, and windproof fleece gloves. Last of all, you put on the goggles that will protect your eyes from the blinding glare of the sunlight bouncing off the snow. (Out here, snow blindness is a real danger. It is extremely painful, like sunburn on your eyeballs.) You unzip the door to your tent and step outside.

The sun is shining brightly, as it has been all night long. Overhead is a clear, blue sky. Aside from the white mountains in the distance, all you can see is snow, ice, and the tents of your fellow workers. There are no birds singing, no flies buzzing, no squirrels chattering. Your world is quiet. The only sound you hear is the crunch of your boots on the snow. Welcome to life in an Antarctic field camp!

A Singular Site for Research

Scientists from around the world come to Antarctica to do research they cannot do anywhere else. Here, the largest ocean current on the planet circles the continent and the surrounding sea ice. It affects not only Antarctica's climate, but also that of the entire planet. Scientists study the atmosphere high above the continent for signs of damage to the environment. Antarctica's thick ice sheets

Most scientists live in Antarctica for a few months out of the year. This is one of the buildings used as temporary housing.

hold clues to the history of Earth's climate. Scientists compare the chemicals deposited deep in ancient ice with newer ice to help predict future climate changes.

The high elevation and clear, dry atmosphere make Antarctica one of the best places on Earth for astrophysicists to peer deep into outer space. Its covering of ice and snow makes Antarctica by far the best place on Earth to search for and spot meteorites, including some from the moon and Mars.

Biologists come to Antarctica to learn how living things adapt to such an extreme environment. Fossil hunters uncover clues about the life that once flourished in Antarctica. And that, as they say, is just the tip of the iceberg.

The Discovery of Antarctica

The great explorer Captain James Cook sailed around Antarctica in 1775, but bad weather and ice prevented him from discovering land. Later, he wrote that if another explorer should find the southern land he sought, "I make bold to declare that the world will derive no benefit from it."[1] Captain Cook would probably be very surprised to learn that many scientists today think of Antarctica as a very cool kind of paradise.

Cook may have thought that whatever land might lie to the south of the icy waters he sailed was of "no benefit," but his descriptions of the many marine animals he saw there caught the attention of whale and seal hunters. The oil from whales and elephant seals was useful for making candles, soap, and fuel for lamps and heating. Other kinds of seals were valued for their soft, thick fur. It was not long before hunters followed in the wake of Cook's ship, killing millions of seals from the islands near Antarctica.

As the seals grew scarcer, the hunters ventured ever closer to the continent. The first recorded landing on Antarctica took place in 1821. Men from an American sealing ship landed at what is now called Hughes Bay, on the western side of the Antarctic Peninsula. The captain of the ship, John Davis, correctly guessed that this new land was not another island, but a continent.

By the end of the nineteenth century, there were few fur or elephant seals left in the Southern Ocean. Commercial seal hunting was all but over. Whale hunting, though, continued well into the twentieth century. Whales are no longer plentiful in the Southern Ocean, but the seal populations have since recovered.

Some of the nineteenth-century whale and seal hunters, to their credit, were also amateur scientists. Others carried professional scientists aboard their ships to collect specimens and make observations. The scientists' reports made the rest of the world hungry for more information about this icy land. While the whalers and sealers did terrible damage to the seal and whale populations around Antarctica, they also paved the way for future scientific exploration on the frozen continent.

Captain James Cook was a British explorer who was one of the first to sail across the Antarctic Circle.

"These Rough Notes and Our Dead Bodies Must Tell the Tale"

Antarctic scientists and explorers endured many hardships in the early years. In 1897 a group of explorers under the command of a Belgian naval officer named Adrien de Gerlache set out for Antarctica. They were not searching for seals or whales. They simply wanted to learn more about this mysterious continent.

In 1898 their ship became trapped in the thickening pack ice. They were forced to spend the winter on their ship. One crewmember had already died by being washed overboard during a storm. There was not enough food for the crew. The food they did have was lacking in vitamin C. Many of the crew developed scurvy; one man died from the disease. They did not have enough warm clothing, and many of the men suffered from mental illness. Frederick Cook, the ship's doctor, wrote, "We are imprisoned in an endless sea of ice, and find our horizon monotonous. We have told all the tales, real and imaginative, to which we are equal. Time weighs heavily upon us as the darkness slowly advances. The despairing storms and the increasing cold call for some new fuel to keep the lowering fires of our bodies ablaze."[2]

Thirteen months after being trapped in the pack ice, the ship finally broke free. Despite the difficulties, they gathered important scientific data about the Antarctic seasons. The ship's first mate, Roald Amundsen, would put the lessons he learned to good use in a later expedition.

In 1911 two rival teams of explorers set out from the Ross Sea. They were each attempting to be the first to reach the geographic South Pole. The Norwegian team, led by Amundsen, traveled using sledges and dog teams. They planted their flag at the pole on December 14, 1911.

British explorer Robert Scott and his team were not as well-prepared for the grueling journey. The men hauled their own sledges over miles of snow and dangerous glaciers. They finally reached the pole on January 17, 1912, only to discover Amundsen's tent and the Norwegian flag. Their hearts sank. Short of food and delayed by unusually severe storms, Scott and his team died on the return trip. In one of the last entries in his journal, Scott wrote, "Had we lived, I should have had a tale to tell of hardihood, endurance, and courage of my companions, which would have stirred the heart of every Englishman. These rough notes and our dead bodies must tell the tale."[3]

One of the most incredible stories of survival in Antarctic history began in 1915. Ernest Shackleton and his crew of twenty-seven men wanted to become the first people to cross the Antarctic continent on foot. But as they made their way to the continent, their ship, the *Endurance*, became trapped in the pack ice of the Weddell Sea. Eighty-five miles (137 kilometers) from land, the ice finally crushed their ship. The ship sank, leaving the crew stranded on the ice floes. Shackleton and his men hauled and rowed their lifeboats to a barren place called Elephant Island. From there, Shackleton and five other men set out in a 22-foot (7-meter) lifeboat to cross nearly 800 miles (1,300 kilometers) of one of the world's stormiest seas to South Georgia Island. Their plan was to get help at a whaling station on the island. Starving, frostbitten, and in tatters, the men had to hike 26 miles (42 kilometers) across mountains and glaciers to reach the station. Finally, twenty-one months after the *Endurance* had set sail, Shackleton returned to rescue the rest of his men from Elephant Island. Not one member of the twenty-eight-man crew was lost.

Throughout the twentieth century, different countries claimed parts of Antarctica as their own. But in 1959, twelve countries signed a treaty that placed all these claims on hold. Today, Antarctica is the only continent not ruled by any nations. The treaty, eventually signed by forty-six countries, says that the continent of Antarctica must never be used for military purposes. No country can make use of its oil or mineral resources. The treaty encourages nations to cooperate on scientific research there. Antarctica is, for the time being at least, a global park for science.

Life on the Icy Continent

Seasons do not exist in Antarctica—at least in the way we think of them. As the earth moves around the sun on its yearly journey, it spins on its axis, tilting to one side. This is why, in North America, there are longer daylight hours in the summer and shorter daylight hours in the

Fast Facts: Antarctic Ice

- Nearly 100 percent of Antarctica is covered by ice— glaciers up to three miles thick.

- Antarctica's glaciers account for 90 percent of the world's ice and 70 percent of all the freshwater in the world.

- Despite all of the ice, the inner part of Antarctica is one of the driest places on earth.

- In the winter, the ocean around the coast freezes in a belt 300 to 900 miles (500 to 1500 kilometers) wide. This doubles the size of the continent.

- Floating ice shelves form about one-third of the coast-line. The largest of these is the Ross Ice Shelf. It is about the size of France.

winter. But at the North and South Poles, the daylight patterns are really extreme!

During Antarctica's summer—from late October through the beginning of February—the sun never sets. (The Antarctic Peninsula is an exception, because it is north of the Antarctic Circle.) During these months, about four thousand people from around the world live and work in Antarctica and on the surrounding islands. By late February, a two-month twilight begins. Most of the scientists and workers return to their homes.

During the long, dark winter, the ice and bitter cold makes travel into or out of most Antarctic stations nearly impossible. The extremely cold winter temperature makes aircraft fuel as thick as jelly. The mechanical parts

Sir Ernest Shackleton was an Irish-born explorer who led three British expeditions to the Antarctic at the start of the twentieth century.

of planes and other vehicles don't work. The weather can be very unstable, with dangerously high winds in the spring. Only around a thousand scientists and support people ("winter-overs") remain, scattered among the continent's bases. Most of the scientific fieldwork comes to a stop. Everyone is happy to see the sun begin to peek over the horizon around the end of August.

Thirty countries operate research stations in Antarctica. Some stations are permanent; others are open only during the summer months. The United States owns three year-round bases in Antarctica. They are called McMurdo Station, the Amundsen-Scott South Pole Station, and Palmer Station.

McMurdo Station, built on Ross Island, is the largest base on the entire continent. It is the hub of the US Antarctic research program. For many scientists, McMurdo is simply the first stop on their way to more remote—and primitive—research camps. Other scientists stay at McMurdo and take day trips to nearby research sites.

McMurdo is a busy place in the summer, when there may be as many as 1,200 people living there. Planes, helicopters, and other vehicles come and go at all hours. When the weather gets "warm" (as high as 36°F [2°C] or more during December), the dark volcanic rock beneath McMurdo heats up. The snow melts, and McMurdo becomes muddy and messy, earning it a new nickname: "McMudhole." By January, the melted snow disappears, and residents like to call it "McDustbowl."[4] By late

Fast Facts: Antarctica

The Antarctic continent is 1.5 times the size of the United States. The Transantarctic Mountain Range crosses the continent, dividing the ice sheet into two parts.

The average annual temperature of the interior part of the continent is –71ºF (–57ºC). The lowest temperature ever recorded on Earth, –128.6ºF (–89ºC), was recorded at a Russian research station in Antarctica. Along the Antarctic Peninsula, temperatures may reach as high as 59ºF (15ºC).

The windiest place on Earth is at Antarctica's Commonwealth Bay, where the average annual wind speed is fifty miles (eighty kilometers) per hour.

Antarctica's largest strictly land animal is a gnat-like insect: It grows to half an inch long. But the coasts and coastal waters are teeming with larger animals. There are invertebrates (animals without spines) like sponges, corals, sea squirts, sea stars, and sea urchins. Penguins, seals, whales, and fish are also plentiful.

Around 200 million years ago, Antarctica was joined to South America, Africa, India, Australia, and New Zealand in one large continent called Gondwana. The weather was mild, and plants and large animals thrived there.

More than 40,000 tourists visit Antarctica each summer. Most of them travel on small cruise ships that travel around the Antarctic Peninsula.

February, the summer visitors have gone home, leaving about 250 hardy winter-overs.

Nearly one thousand miles (1,600 kilometers) south of McMurdo is the Amundsen-Scott South Pole Station. At 9,300 feet (2,800 meters) above sea level, it sits on a 2-mile-thick (3-kilometer-thick) sheet of ice that moves about 33 feet (10 meters) each year. Because of this, scientists move the sign marking the geographic South Pole every January 1.

The South Pole station is also one of the coldest and most isolated places on Earth. A new station was completed in early 2007 to replace the old one. The old

Palmer Station on Anvers Island is the smallest US research base in Antarctica. Many scientists go there to study the abundant wildlife.

station was a huge dome, but the new station is raised on sturdy stilts. Blowing snow can pass under the building or be cleared out by bulldozers. Aside from the station, there is an airplane runway made of packed snow and several scattered research buildings, including a seven-story telescope.

About 260 scientists and support people stay at the South Pole station during the summer months. From February to October, that number drops to around fifty.

Palmer Station, on Anvers Island just off the Antarctic Peninsula, is the smallest US research base. In the summer, there is room for just forty-three scientists and support staff. Only about fifteen to twenty people spend the winter there. Palmer is north of the Antarctic Circle, and it does not get as cold as the rest of the continent. Because of its warmer climate, sometimes people playfully call it the "Banana Belt" of Antarctica. Unlike at the McMurdo and South Pole stations, there is a lot of wildlife at Palmer, making it a popular place to study birds, seals, and other Antarctic animals.

Marine biologists in Antarctica often dive into the coastal waters to study the rich forests of algae and plentiful animals on the sea floor. Other scientists live and work aboard research vessels that cruise the Southern Ocean for weeks at a time.

Most American scientists who go to Antarctica to do research are required to have a complete medical and dental checkup at least six months ahead of time. There are medical clinics in the major stations, but they are not equipped to handle serious medical emergencies. People who want to winter over in Antarctica must undergo mental evaluations as well.

Scientists and station support staff work very hard in Antarctica, but they also have plenty of opportunities for entertainment. Depending on the base, there may be weekly science lectures, music festivals, art shows, comedy nights, footraces, and amateur theater. There are gyms, libraries, and movies.

The winter-overs—many of whom return year after year—have developed some especially creative ways of dealing with the winter doldrums. One of the most bizarre is the "300 Club." This is a South Pole Station tradition that requires its members to experience a 300°F (149°C) temperature difference in a matter of minutes. People wait for the temperature to drop to –100°F (–73°C) outside. They enter the sauna, then crank the heat up to 200°F (93°C) and sit until they get good and toasty. Then, wearing only boots and scarves to cover their mouths, they dash the 100 yards (91 meters) to the South Pole marker, run around it, and head back to the sauna! (People who live at McMurdo, which is warmer than the South Pole, have a 200 Club.)

Chapter 2

Dinosaurs Frozen in Time

In 1991 paleontologist Dr. William Hammer and his team discovered a collection of bones embedded in solid rock.[1] Most of the bones belonged to a previously unknown meat-eating dinosaur, but there were bones from a plant-eating dinosaur, and teeth from other creatures. Bones can tell stories to those who study them, and Hammer is fluent in the language of bones.

This story took place about 190 million years ago, in a riverbed surrounded by lush greenery. A 22-foot (7-meter)-long dinosaur was eating its dinner of prosauropod, a peaceful plant-eating dinosaur. The meat eater was a curious looking creature, something like a small version of *Tyrannosaurus rex*, but with a bizarre furrowed crest running across its head, just over its eyes.

Dinosaurs are not known for their table manners, and this early Jurassic meat eater was no exception. The dinosaur got one of the prosauropod's ribs stuck in its throat, choked, and died. Some time later, small scavenging dinosaurs and a mammal-like creature came along to feast on the big predator. Millions of years later, the rib remained stuck in the bones of the dinosaur's mouth, all the way to the back of its neck. Small scavenging dinosaurs and mammal-like creatures left clues in the form of gnaw marks on the dinosaur's bones and some teeth they lost in the dinosaur's tough hide.

Some version of this scenario must have happened many times in the millions of years that dinosaurs roamed the earth. What makes it really interesting is that it happened in Antarctica, at a time when the continent was much warmer than it is today.

The area had once been a soft riverbed before shifts in the earth's crust pushed it skyward. Hammer later named the dinosaur *Cryolophosaurus ellioti*. (The first half of the name means "frozen-crested reptile." The second half honors David Elliot, the geologist who spotted the first bone.)

Bones in the Rocks

Hammer, a geology professor at Augustana College in Rock Island, Illinois, has been hunting for fossils in Antarctica since 1977. Antarctic fossil hunters are a hardy bunch of scientists. Like everyone who works

Two *Cryolophosaurus ellioti* dinosaurs fight over the dead body of a prosauropod dinosaur. *Cryolophosaurus* roamed Antarctica millions of years ago.

in Antarctica, Hammer and his team spend a week at McMurdo Station before venturing out to their field camp. At McMurdo, they learn how to make snow shelters in case their tents blow away in winds that can gust over thirty-one miles (fifty kilometers) per hour. They learn how to get into and out of crevasses, how to climb up and down ropes, and how to rappel. They learn how to prevent altitude sickness, which can result from the lower oxygen levels at high altitudes.

After receiving all of their extreme weather gear and safety training, the team flies five hundred miles (eight hundred kilometers) south to a glacier in the Transantarctic Mountains. They set up camp on the

Dr. William Hammer looks for fossils in Antarctica near the Beardmore Glacier.

glacier, not because that is where the bones are, but because the weather there is nice. In Antarctica, *nice* is a relative term. Temperatures at their base camp can be as high as 0°F (-18°C). But higher up on the mountain, where the dinosaur bones lay encased in rock, temperatures can plummet to -30°F (-34°C). A helicopter pilot shuttles them back and forth between their base camp and the quarry.

Camping under such conditions is "not much fun," Hammer admits. "Sometimes you have to deal with the fact that you're stuck in a tent for a week. The wind is blowing 50 miles [80 kilometers] per hour, everybody's cold, and there's not much to do besides read."[2]

But for Hammer, the excitement of finding fossils in this frozen continent makes up for the hardship. In his first few trips to the Transantarctic Mountains, he and his colleagues discovered the fossil remains of pre-mammals, called synapsids, and giant amphibians that lived about 250 to 200 million years ago. Because the amphibians did not migrate and could not have survived if the water froze in the winter, their fossils are evidence that Antarctica was once warm.

In the 1991 field season, Hammer and his team had already spent weeks digging reptile and amphibian fossils out of the ice and rock near the base of Mount Kirkpatrick. They were 9,000 feet (2,743 meters) above sea level when they got a call on the shortwave radio. David Elliot, a scientist working on another project, had found a piece of rock with a bone in it. It had fallen

Careers in Paleontology

Paleontology is about more than just dinosaurs. It is the study of the history of life on Earth, looking at the fossil record. Fossils are the remains or traces of living things—animals, plants, fungi, and even microorganisms—that are preserved in Earth's crust. Most paleontologists have a degree in geology or biology, but it is best to study both.

After graduating from college, the next step is to get a master's degree, or preferably, a doctoral degree (PhD) in paleontology. Most paleontologists follow their doctoral degree with postdoctoral research before finding jobs as college or university professors, where they teach as well as do research. Some paleontologists work in museums. Others may work for oil companies, helping to search for petroleum. Paleontologists fall in the category of geoscientists. In 2013 the median yearly salary of a geoscientist was $108,420.[3]

from a site thousands of feet above. They flew up in the helicopter to take a look. There, at 13,000 feet (3,962 m), they discovered the frozen remains of an ancient riverbank. They could clearly see fossils in the stone—lots of them! Hammer knew that getting the bones off the side of the frozen mountain would not be easy. They were encased in extremely hard rock. Hammer and his team used gasoline-powered jackhammers, sledgehammers, and chisels to break off chunks of rock containing the bones. They numbered each block of rock. Later, they

Hammer uncovers fossils in rocks collected on an Antarctic exhibition.

would use the numbers to put the bones back together again. The rocks with their treasures of bones would be carried off the mountain in big slings carried under helicopters.

Breaking up rocks is hard work under any conditions. But there is not as much oxygen in the air at such high altitudes. The thin air makes the scientists tire more quickly than usual. And then, of course, there is the unrelenting cold. The scientists have to make sure they eat and drink enough to keep up their energy levels and to prevent dehydration.

In the end, it took Hammer and his team three weeks to excavate more than 5,000 pounds (2,268 kilograms) of bone-bearing rocks. However, high winds forced them to abandon their site before they could remove all of the fossils. They knew that the hard rock and freezing temperatures would protect the fossils from erosion. And the possibility of bandits coming to plunder the rest of the fossils was extremely unlikely!

Back in his Illinois laboratory, Hammer and his colleagues spent years painstakingly chipping away at the rock encasing the bones. It took nearly a year of full-time work just to free the skull.

It was thirteen years before Hammer and his team could return to finish the excavation. While the team was busy excavating the rest of the *Cryolophosaurus*, their mountain safety guide was exploring an area about 100 feet (30 meters) higher on the mountainside. He spotted two large bones. When he showed them to

Pieces of the Puzzle

It is no coincidence that Africa and South America look like puzzle pieces that should fit together. They, and all of the world's other landmasses, were once one big supercontinent called Pangaea (pan-JEE-uh). Then about 200 million years ago, Pangaea began to break up into two separate continents. Laurasia included most of the continents now found in the northern hemisphere. Gondwana included what is now Africa, South America, India, Australia, and Antarctica. Animals roamed lush forests throughout much of Gondwana. Scientists believe the climate was cool and rather mild—similar to the climate in parts of the United States.

Over millions of years, Gondwana, too, broke apart. Antarctica (with Australia still attached) began to drift south. By sixty-five million years ago, Antarctica was near its present position inside the Antarctic Circle. It was still fairly warm, though, because the entire world was warmer. Still, the plants and animals must have evolved ways of coping with the very short periods of daylight in the winter and the very short nights in the summer. Around forty million years ago, Australia separated from Antarctica, and the first ice began to appear on the southern continent. By fifteen million years ago, the Antarctic ice sheets had become permanent.

The theory that explains the breakup of Pangaea and the movement of continents is called plate tectonics. It was a controversial theory until 1969. That year, paleontologists made an important discovery in Antarctica. The scientists found the remains of an early Triassic animal, *Lystrosaurus*. An ancestor of mammals, this plant-eating animal lived in herds near lakes and swamps. Since fossils of the animal had been found in South Africa, India, Europe, and Asia, this discovery gave a big boost to the theory of plate tectonics. *Lystrosaurus* was not a good swimmer, so it must have walked on land to get to what is now Antarctica. And it could only have done that if all of the land masses were once connected to each other.

A map of the ancient world shows the positions of the landmasses during the Paleozoic and Mesozoic eras. At one point, all of these areas were one giant continent known as Pangaea.

Scott Base is a scientific research center on Ross Island in Antarctica. It accommodates about eighty people during the summer months.

Hammer, there was no doubt about it. They were part of an enormous pelvis!

Hammer and the other scientists dug out the pelvis, then vertebrae and parts of legs. Getting the bones off the mountain was tricky. The helicopter pilot had to land on a rocky ledge, and then take off carrying several thousand pounds of rock-encased fossils in an attached sling.

That dinosaur turned out to be a primitive sauropod—a big, long-necked, long-tailed plant-eating dinosaur. Even though it must have weighed somewhere between 4 and 6 tons (3.6–5.4 metric tons), spanning

Brachiosaurus is one example of a sauropod, some of the largest creatures to walk the earth. The sauropod discovered by Hammer, *Glacialisaurus hammeri*, was tiny by comparison to other sauropods.

20 to 25 feet (6–7 meters) from head to tail, it was "kind of wimpy for a sauropod," Hammer said.[4] (Some sauropods reached 100 feet or 30 meters in length.) It may be small, but it is very old: 190 million years. The dinosaur's very fitting name: *Glacialisaurus hammeri* (Hammer's ice lizard).

Antarctica may not be the easiest place to hunt for dinosaurs, but it is exciting. The new discoveries just keep on coming. In the 2010–2011 season, Hammer's team found the bones of two previously undiscovered primitive sauropods. One was a nearly complete skeleton—so small that the scientists knew it must have been a baby. "We have so few dinosaur specimens from [Antarctica] compared to any other place, that almost anything we find down there is new to science," Hammer said.[5]

A Surprise on Ross Island

In late November 2003, a team of paleontologists working in Antarctica made a remarkable discovery. Just off the coast of the Antarctic Peninsula in the Weddell Sea, Judd Case, James Martin, and their research team found the remains of a new species of dinosaur on James Ross Island.

The scientists had been headed for Vega Island, where they had found the remains of a duck-billed dinosaur a few years earlier. They hoped to find evidence that marsupials (pouched mammals like kangaroos and opossums), or their ancestors, once lived there. But icebergs made it impossible to reach the island. Disappointed, they set up camp on nearby James Ross Island instead. They thought they might find some marine reptiles on a peninsula called the Naze, four miles from their campsite.

Each day, the scientists made the long hike from their camp to the Naze. They worked in snowy whiteout conditions with only the occasional sunny day, finding very few fossils for all their efforts.

Their luck changed on December 12. They stumbled upon some very puzzling bones. Although they knew that the area they were searching had once been deep under the Weddell Sea, these were the bones of a land creature, a dinosaur! Later, they determined that the dinosaur had stood about six to eight feet tall and was a meat eater, related to tyrannosaurs and velociraptors. The dinosaur had probably died on land and washed out to sea about seventy million years ago. The creature's teeth and leg bones told the researchers that it was much more primitive than other, related dinosaurs of that period. As is often the case with science, the discovery of this strange new dinosaur raised new questions.

"One of the surprising things is that animals with these more primitive characteristics generally haven't survived as long elsewhere as they have in Antarctica," Case said. "For whatever reason, they are still hanging out on the Antarctic continent. Why is this group still here when in other places other groups have displaced them? We don't know."[6]

Chapter 3

Space Rocks (on Earth)

A robot the size of a car roams the dusty surface of Mars, searching for signs of life. Nobody expects the robot, named the Curiosity Rover, to find little green men, but it's possible that Mars may have once supported microbes. In 2020, the National Aeronautics and Space Administration (NASA) will launch a new robot to Mars. Scientists hope to send the robot to an interesting region called Nili Fossae, where lava from a huge volcano eruption once ran over land. There might be clues to life on Mars hiding under that lava!

Dr. Ralph Harvey is one of those scientists eager to learn the secrets of those Martian volcano rocks— because he has collected and studied meteorites that might well have come from that very place. When Harvey was a boy, he dreamed of becoming an astronaut. The

United States and the Soviet Union were competing in a race to explore outer space. The Soviet Union sent the first man into outer space in 1961. American astronauts Neil Armstrong and Edwin "Buzz" Aldrin were the first people to set foot on the moon. Like millions of others, Harvey was fascinated by the idea of exploring worlds beyond our own. His favorite toy was an astronaut figure, Major Matt Mason. "I thought I'd be putting on a rocket pack and flying to the moon for lunch," he said.[1]

NASA's rover *Curiosity* took this self-portrait on Mars in 2013.

But when Harvey reached his teens in the mid-1970s, space exploration began to slow down. The United States and the Soviet Union began to cooperate, rather than compete, in space missions. Money for the space programs dwindled, and Harvey's dream of exploring the solar system faded. He went to college and studied geology. He learned how rocks, soil, and minerals hold clues to the formation and history of Earth. When he graduated from college, he wanted to learn more about the geology of other planets, so he went to graduate school to earn a PhD (doctor of philosophy) in geology.

While he was in graduate school, Harvey was offered the chance to go to Antarctica to hunt for meteorites—pieces of rock or metal from asteroids, the moon, or even Mars—that fall to Earth from outer space. He almost turned it down! Fortunately, he accepted. It was a choice that changed his life.

Now a professor of geology at Case Western Reserve University in Cleveland, Ohio, Harvey has returned to Antarctica nearly every year since 1987. He and other members of the Antarctic Search for Meteorites (ANSMET) team have collected thousands of meteorites from the ice.

The East Antarctic Ice Sheet may seem an unlikely place for a scientist to find meteorites, but as far as Harvey and his colleagues are concerned, Antarctica is the ideal place to search for these messengers from outer space.

Meteorites land evenly all over the earth. Most fall in the ocean. Others fall on rocky places where they can be hard to spot. Still others become buried under layers of soil. "If you want to find things that fall from the sky," Harvey said, "the best place is Antarctica's big, white ice sheet. If you find any rocks there, they've got to be meteorites."

Harvey also explained that, as snow collects on the ice sheet, the snow's weight pushes the sheet toward the edges of the continent. The ice sheet acts like a conveyor belt, delivering meteorites that have fallen over tens of thousands of years to the base of the Transantarctic Mountains. Over time, the ice surface evaporates, uncovering meteorites buried under the ice. This is where Harvey and his colleagues on the ANSMET team focus their search for meteorites.

Life in a Snow Globe

Each November, the ANSMET team flies to Christchurch, New Zealand, where they are outfitted for their expedition. They receive long underwear, fleece shirts and pants, heavy wind pants, down-filled parkas, double-insulated boots, goggles, hats, neck warmers, mittens, and gloves. In Christchurch, they board a cargo airplane for the eight-hour flight to McMurdo Station. If the weather is bad, they must turn around in mid-flight and return to New Zealand until the weather improves.

Once at McMurdo Station, team members are required to take the Antarctic survival training course,

Dr. Ralph Harvey poses with a large meteorite.

A Giant Crater Under Ice

Hidden deep below the ice in East Antarctica, planetary scientists have discovered what appears to be a huge crater. It is roughly the size of Ohio. The scientists speculate that a meteorite up to thirty miles (forty-eight kilometers) wide crashed into the Wilkes Land region of Antarctica around 250 million years ago. It could have caused nearly all of the animal life on Earth to die out. The Wilkes Land crater is more than twice the size of the crater in Mexico that marks the impact of a meteorite believed to have killed the dinosaurs sixty-five million years ago. The impact of such a large meteorite might even have begun the breakup of Gondwana.

Scientists discovered the crater by studying data from a space satellite.[2] The structure is buried under more than a mile of ice. Ralph von Frese, the lead scientist on the study, would like to go to Antarctica to confirm whether it really is a meteorite crater. The best evidence would come from rocks within the crater. To get to these rocks, scientists would have to drill through more than a mile of ice. That would be too expensive. Instead, they plan to hunt for rocks pushed to the coast by glaciers.

jokingly referred to as "Happy Campers' School." Then they fly out to the East Antarctic plateau and set up camp. This will be their home for the next four to five weeks. They live in Scott tents, modeled after the tents that Robert Scott used on his polar expeditions. Unlike Scott's camp, however, the modern camp has electricity, provided by solar panels and a wind generator. Electricity allows the scientists to communicate with McMurdo and to recharge their computers and other equipment.

Two people can comfortably share a tent. Boxes of frozen food are stored outside the tents. The scientists use camp stoves to cook and to warm their shelters, using a chimney at the top to let the fumes out. With the stove going, a tent can be quite cozy, even though the temperature outside hovers around –4°F (–20°C). Their biggest daily chore is collecting and melting ice for their water.

If you have ever camped, you probably sought out a protected area to pitch your tent. The meteorite hunters camp in areas that are very windy and exposed. Because the wind speeds up the evaporation of the snow and ice, these are the most likely places to find meteorites. About one out of every three days it is too windy to work outside. The scientists must hunker down in their tents and wait until the weather improves. To pass the time, they read books, play games, or listen to music.

On one such windy day, Harvey wrote a note to his sons back home: "The snow hits your face like little needles, gets in under your clothes and sunglasses, making it a little uncomfortable to be outside. I feel like I'm in a snow globe that someone is shaking very hard."[3]

The Rock Hunt

When the weather cooperates, the ANSMET teams head out on the ice to look for meteorites. A four-person team scouts out the best sites to search. An eight-person team follows to collect the meteorites. The team members drive their snowmobiles across a selected patch of ice, slowly crisscrossing the area in overlapping paths until they are sure that human eyes have scanned every inch of the area. Occasionally they hit a rocky spot. When they do, they leave their snowmobiles behind and scour the area on foot. "It's kind of like a sophisticated Easter egg hunt," Harvey says.

Spotting the meteorites, even among earth rocks, is not as hard as it might seem. The ANSMET team members are trained to recognize meteorites. "Anybody can learn how to pick out which rock is unusual," Harvey said. "You don't have to be a geologist."

Meteorites burn as they enter Earth's atmosphere, so many of them have a black or dark brown crust, like charcoal. They are very dense. Most contain at least some iron. Some appear to have thumbprints, as if someone pressed a thumb into a piece of clay. Some may be small pebbles. Others are more like boulders, weighing as much as seventy pounds (thirty-two kilograms). Most meteorites are around the size of a baseball or golf ball.

Once the team members find a meteorite, they locate its position using a Global Positioning System (GPS) device. They describe it, give it an identification number, and use tongs to put it into a sterile bag. The meteorite will stay frozen throughout its journey back to the National Aeronautics and Space Administration (NASA) Johnson Space Center in Houston, Texas.

Harvey and his ANSMET colleagues do not get to keep the meteorites they find. Instead, the precious rocks from outer space are kept at the Smithsonian Institution in Washington, D.C. Geologists there analyze small chunks of the meteorites to find out what they are made of, which can help determine where they came from. Scientists from all over the world can request samples to

Careers in Geology

Many geologists teach and carry out research for colleges and universities. Others work for the government or for companies, especially oil and gas firms. It is common for geologists to work in remote field sites, in all kinds of weather. This typically involves a field course or two, usually in the mountains.

You will need to study geology or a field related to earth science in college. After you earn your college degree, you will need to go to graduate school for more specialized coursework and research in geology. Most geologists need at least a master of science degree; but high-level research and college teaching positions usually require a PhD and postdoctoral research experience. The median annual earnings of geoscientists in 2013 was $108,420.[4]

"What almost no one tells young people," said Harvey, "is that if you can get through your college years, most of you can go to graduate school for free." Scientists usually receive scholarships and tuition support, and even get paid to teach laboratory courses.

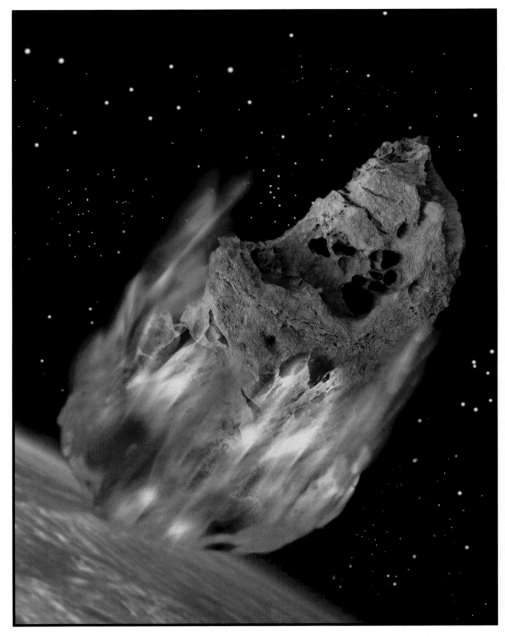

A meteorite is a piece of debris that has broken off from a space object like a comet or asteroid and hits the earth. Scientists look for meteorites in Antarctica where they are relatively easy to find.

study in their own laboratories. Since 1976, more than ten thousand samples have been sent to hundreds of scientists all over the world.

During the 2006–2007 field season, Harvey's teams found 856 meteorites—a bumper crop compared to the average haul of about 500![5]

Hunting for meteorites is hard work. "You have to be physically and mentally qualified," Harvey said. "I vet my applicants carefully. I want people who have the required physical and mental toughness, but my shining guiding light is a sense of humor. That can get you through a lot."

Valuable Clues From Space Trash

Have you ever seen a shooting star? Perhaps you made a wish upon the bright streak of light as it soared through the night sky. Actually, a shooting star is not a star at all. Those brilliant flashes of light in the night sky are called meteors. They are created when meteoroids (rocks orbiting the sun) fall into Earth's atmosphere, 50 to 70 miles (80 to 112 kilometers) above its surface. As the meteoroids move through the atmosphere, they heat up and burn. Those that do not burn up completely eventually hit the earth. These are called meteorites.

Meteorites are like free rock samples from outer space. They are the debris that was left over from the rough-and-tumble period of our solar system's birth. Evidence shows that asteroids—rocky bodies in space ranging in size from a few hundred feet to several hundred miles across—smashed into each other. Chunks of rock flew everywhere. These chunks, the meteoroids, are like time capsules. They contain information from billions of years ago, clues to the formation of the solar system.

Occasionally, the meteorite hunters will find pieces of the moon or Mars, created by the impact of an asteroid or comet. Of the 24,000 or so meteorites found on Earth, only 34 apparently came from Mars. Eleven of these were found in Antarctica.[6] In 2004 members of the ANSMET team found a fist-sized Martian meteorite. It was probably formed during a volcanic eruption on Mars. It is also among the oldest of all Martian meteorites, and that makes it particularly valuable to scientists. By studying the chemical makeup of the rock and the gases trapped inside, geologists can learn about the history of the planet. "The rock has potentially recorded not only a volcanic event 1.3 billion years ago, but all of the ensuing activity on Mars," Harvey said.[7]

"The study of other planets and asteroids is in its infancy," Harvey said. "We know that there are huge gaps in our knowledge about other planets, and about how our solar system was formed. That's why it is so important to study meteorites."

Harvey will never put on his rocket pack and fly to the moon, but that is fine with him. "I'm doing something very close to what I had always dreamed of doing," he said. "I am exploring other worlds, and picking up aliens. It's an amazing thrill to be the earth's alien dogcatcher."

Chapter 4

A Big Job for Tiny Worms

Visitors to Antarctica's McMurdo Dry Valleys might well think that they are the only living creatures around. There are no other animals. There are no plants. It is 1,853 square miles (4,800 km²) of cold, dry desert: a vast expanse of dirt, frozen lakes, and the occasional short-lived summer stream. What little snow falls usually evaporates before it hits the ground.

When Robert Falcon Scott discovered Antarctica's Taylor Valley in 1903, he described it as a "valley of the dead." "We have seen no living thing, not even a moss or a lichen," Scott wrote in *The Voyage of the Discovery*, his book about the journey.[1]

As it turns out, the Dry Valleys contain more life than most of the Antarctic mainland. Only the peninsula has more living creatures. But Scott may be excused for his mistake, because he did not have a microscope.

The Dry Valleys are home to microscopic animals that feed on bacteria and algae. There are mites, related to the creatures that plague our pets and live in our house dust. They are joined by water bears, so called because they resemble miniature eight-legged bears. There are also tiny worms called nematodes. Tiny springtails fling themselves into the air with their tails. More than a century after Scott's observation, biologist E.O. Wilson wrote of the Dry Valleys: "At the top of this rarefied food web are four species of nematode worms. . . .With the mites and springtails they are also the largest of the animals, McMurdo's equivalent of elephants and tigers, yet all but invisible to the naked eye."[2]

Enter Dr. Diana Wall and her fellow scientists, nicknamed "worm herders." Wall, a soil ecologist at Colorado State University in Fort Collins, first came to the Dry Valleys in 1989. She was not sure whether she would find anything—but she found nematodes galore! She has returned to the Valleys every summer since to study McMurdo's microscopic elephants and tigers—especially one nematode critical to the ecosystem. And, by learning more about how climate change affects this bare-bones food web, she hopes to understand how warming global temperatures might affect more complex food webs around the world.

Mars? No, Antarctica

It is a forty-minute helicopter ride from McMurdo Station to Taylor Valley. The landscape there is so barren

Dr. Diana Wall (left), standing with colleague Dr. Ross Virginia, studies microscopic life in Antarctica.

Parasites? No, Thanks!

Like many ecologists, Wall has always loved the outdoors. As a girl, she spent a lot of time exploring the Kentucky hills around her home. When she got older, she studied biology in college. One summer, she got a research job in a laboratory looking at human and horse parasites.

Studying horse parasites could be a smelly business, though. When she went to graduate school, she decided to study plant parasites. There she read a book about free-living nematodes that really grabbed her attention. These were the good guys, she thought, but no one really paid them much attention. After she received her PhD in plant pathology, she began to study the "good guys."

that the scientists could well imagine that the pilot had taken a wrong turn and delivered them to Mars instead. The main reason the Dry Valleys are ice-free is that the Transantarctic Mountains form a kind of dam, holding back the East Antarctic Ice Sheet. The glaciers that manage to creep through a few narrow gaps in the mountains cannot advance far. Strong winds from the mountains immediately sublimate the ice; that is, the winds change the solid ice into a gas form.

Wall and her colleagues visit Taylor Valley in the Antarctic summer, when the sun and rising temperatures (just above freezing) cause the glaciers to melt—if only a little. The summer's short-lived streams are the only source of water for the ecosystem.

Most of the time, the nematode scientists are day-trippers. They spend the day in the valley collecting samples, and then fly back to McMurdo that same day to study the soil. Like other researchers in the Dry Valleys, they know how important it is to preserve the pristine environment. "We're really aware of dropping candy bars and getting crumbs on the soil," Wall says, "because that's an added source of carbon."[3] Every person has a pee bottle as well as a poop sack for use in the field!

Scientists pour water into chambers to wet the soil below. This is part of an experiment to look at the effect of global warming on nematodes in the soil.

Lake Vida's Ancient Life

Antarctica has at least 145 lakes (and probably many more) trapped beneath blankets of ice up to 2.5 miles (4 kilometers) thick. We would find these lakes to be an awfully chilly home, but there are living microbes in the ice—and in the water below. These microbes are so extreme that scientists regard them as examples of what life on Mars might be like.

John Priscu, an ecology professor at Montana State University, and his colleagues discovered 2,800-year-old bacteria and algae frozen in the ice cover of Lake Vida, one of the largest lakes in the McMurdo Dry Valleys.[4] When the microbes were thawed in some water, they were successfully revived!

On a return visit to Antarctica, Priscu set his sights on a lake trapped under a thick ice sheet. He and his team drilled down through (2,600 feet) 800 meters of ice before reaching water. They collected samples of

Wall and the other scientists found just four species of nematodes in the valley. By comparison, a handful of dirt from a Kansas prairie might yield hundreds of species of nematodes, not to mention millions of other types of microscopic creatures, bacteria, and fungi. Trying to understand the role each species plays in such a complicated ecosystem would be impossible. The simple food web in Taylor Valley makes it a perfect laboratory for studying interactions between living things.

water and mud from the bottom of the lake. When they put their samples under the microscope, they found what they'd been hoping for: living microbes. The strange microbes live in complete darkness, because the sun's rays cannot penetrate all that ice. They get their energy from chemicals in the mud and water.

If there is—or was—life on Mars, it might look like the critters found in Antarctic lakes. Peter Doran, a researcher on the project, said, "Mars is believed to have a water-rich past, and if life developed, a Lake Vida-type ecosystem may have been the final niche for life on Mars before the water bodies froze solid."[5] Jupiter's moon Europa is thought to have a large underground ocean of water that might also be home to similar microbes. "I always tell my students when they come into the lab that 'We are inventing this field of science. It's working on life in ice and under ice. This field has never existed before. We thought it up. You are pioneers,'" Priscu said.[6]

The hardiest and most abundant nematode species in the valley, *Scottnema lindsayae*, is found only in Antarctica. *S. lindsayae* thrives in the driest, saltiest areas, feasting on bacteria and yeast. "It's a Rambo-like thing," Wall said. "It's not ugly, but it's a really tough-looking nematode."[7] The other three species of nematodes need more water. They live near melt streams or frozen lakes. All four species survive the nine-month winter by drying up, losing 99 percent of their water. Coiled up

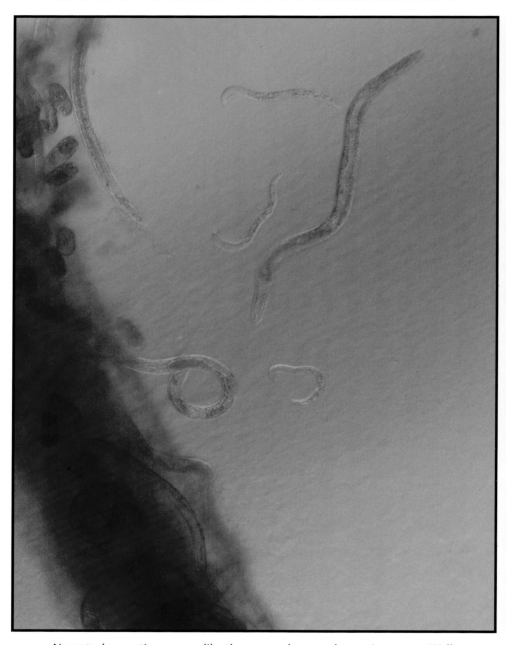

Nematodes are tiny worms like those seen here under a microscope. Wall studies the few species that live in Antarctica to better understand their role in the ecosystem.

like tiny donuts, they lie as if in suspended animation. They awaken only when the spring melt brings them back to life.

To study these little creatures, Wall's team collects soil samples from across the valley, placing them in carefully labeled bags. They bring their samples back to the lab

(!) Worms, Worms Everywhere

Nematodes are the most numerous animals on Earth. Scientists have identified nearly 20,000 species, living in just about every environment imaginable. Many nematodes are parasites that can cause diseases in plants or animals. If you have a dog, you probably take it to the vet for a shot to protect it against heartworm, an especially nasty parasitic nematode.

But many other nematodes are "good guys." They make soil more fertile by speeding up decomposition and decay. They recycle nutrients into forms that plants can use. These nematodes and other soil creatures are essential for healthy, productive soils.

at McMurdo—very gently, Wall said, because they do not want to squash the nematodes. Within twenty-four hours of collecting the samples, the scientists begin to process them. They measure the amount of water and nutrients in the soil. They wash the nematodes and any other creatures from the dirt and count them under the microscope: living, dead, adults, babies, male, and female.

Careers in Ecology

Ecologists study the relationship between the environment and things that influence it, including rainfall, temperature shifts, pollution, and human activity. Ecologists may spend weeks or even months doing fieldwork each year. Most ecologists are scientists with backgrounds in chemistry, environmental science, geology, biology, climatology, and statistics. In 2013 the median salary of environmental scientists was $70,770.[8]

Most ecologists need at least a master's degree to do research. A PhD, followed by a one- to two-year postdoctoral position is usually required to teach and do research at a university or college.

What is Wall's advice for a budding soil ecologist? "Find what's interesting to you, and keep exploring the options. The soil is a natural resource, and we know so little about it," she said. "I just think it's the most exciting field right now, and it's so important to the environment. We're aware that water and air can become polluted, but we don't pay enough attention to the wonderful biodiversity that's below our feet. I think that science is like a playpen; research is fantastic. There are so many questions, and you have the feeling that you can do something useful. I think that's so critical for us right now."

Wall has seen some striking changes in the valley's nematode population since she began studying it in 1993. Rising temperatures and melting ice in the Dry Valleys have made the soil a friendlier environment to a competing nematode. The *Scottnema* nematode, on the other hand, has declined 65 percent in the past few years.[9] Wall thinks this could have a dramatic effect on the chemistry and nutrients in the soil. The creature that shoulders the greatest burden in recycling soil nutrients, Wall says, "is one species that is crashing and burning."[10]

Does the decline of one tiny worm in an Antarctic desert really matter? Wall believes it does. Soils around the world are being hit hard by global climate change, land use, and pollution. The soils "are the reason we have a food breadbasket," she says. "By studying this simple species and its response to climate change in the Dry Valleys, we now have a better picture of what might be happening in more complex systems."[11]

Chapter 5

Secrets of the Glaciers

One of the first things visitors to the McMurdo Dry Valleys of Antarctica notice is the silence. There are no dogs barking, no birds singing, no car horns honking. The wind sometimes howls. For a few weeks in the summer, when the temperature hovers around the freezing mark and the sun shines twenty-four hours a day, there is the sound of trickling water as nearby glaciers slowly melt. They creak and groan as they shift in place.

"The meltwater flow from the glaciers is the only source of water to the ecosystem in the valley," says Dr. Andrew Fountain, associate professor of geography and geology at Portland State University in Oregon. "To understand the ecosystem, you have to understand how the water melts from the glaciers."[1]

Fountain has been studying the glaciers of Taylor Valley since 1993. That year, he joined a team of scientists (including Wall) to study the ecosystem of that cold, dry desert. But in a larger sense, he also seeks to understand how Earth's changing climate affects glaciers around the world.

Life at the Lake Hoare Field Camp

Most of the glaciers on Earth, including those in Europe and North America, are shrinking at a rapid rate. Scientists, including Fountain, widely agree that these glaciers are the victims of global climate change. He has estimated that if the warming trend continues, most of the glaciers in the Western United States will disappear in the next 50 to 250 years.[2] Glacier National Park in Montana will have glaciers in name only.

But when Fountain compared photographs of the Dry Valley glaciers taken in the 1970s with more recent photographs, he found that they were staying the same or even moving forward. Why should the Dry Valley glaciers be different? Are they actually growing and gaining mass, or is something else happening? Fountain hopes to answer these questions. And so, year after year, he returns to the Dry Valleys to measure the ice levels of glaciers.

Fountain and his colleagues typically spend a few weeks each summer at the Lake Hoare field camp, near glaciers as tall as six-story buildings. Compared to many other Antarctic field camps, theirs is fairly comfortable.

Dr. Andrew Fountain (right) and a colleague hike to Canada Glacier.

Fountain sleeps in his own tent, and when he wakes, he makes a note of the place where the sun hits his tent. The sun has been shining all night long, of course, but its movement across the sky gives him a good idea of the time. He dresses and walks to the main hut, warmed by diesel-fueled heaters. Solar panels and a generator bring power to the hut.

Over hearty breakfasts of coffee, eggs, and cereal, he and his colleagues plan their day. They write their plans on a common board: where they are going, how they can be contacted, and what time they plan to come back. That way, if they are overdue, someone can come rescue them. Those who live and work in this harsh land do not leave anything to chance.

The scientists may spend one hour hiking to the top of a neighboring glacier. If the day's work is farther away, they fly in a helicopter. Their goal is to measure the amounts of ice on the glaciers.

Their methods are surprisingly low-tech. Fountain and his colleagues stick bamboo poles into holes drilled into the glacier. Then they measure the stakes over the course of a season. A shorter stake indicates that the glacier is gaining ice. A longer one shows that it is losing ice. They also monitor weather stations installed on the glaciers. The data will help them understand how weather conditions affect the amount of ice.

Fountain also wants to know *how* the glaciers melt. It is not as simple as it might seem! Even as the ever-present sun warms the ice, the dry winds blowing over

Two researchers measure the snow density and stake height of Canada Glacier.

the surface of the glacier sublimate the ice before it even gets a chance to melt. Instead, the ice often melts in pockets beneath the surface. Fountain uses probes to measure these pools of water. Working with the biologists and chemists on the team, he samples the water for microorganisms and measures the water chemistry.

The scientists spend the day walking around the glacier, collecting data. They stop only to eat the lunch they have packed. Fountain likes to add a freeze-dried meal to a thermos of hot water. "It warms you right up," he says. The research is not terribly difficult work, but there are loads of things to remember and procedures to follow. The scientists are not bored, surrounded as they are by the starkly beautiful landscape and the long shadows cast by the sun that circles low in the sky.

Back at the camp, Fountain and his colleagues analyze data, relax, and get some well-deserved rest. They will need it for another day of work on the glacier. After a few weeks in the Dry Valleys, Fountain will return to the relative warmth of his laboratory back home in Portland to study and further analyze the data.

Fascinated by Ice

Back in his laboratory in Portland, Fountain uses computer models, photographs, and the data he collected to understand the Dry Valley glaciers. The glaciers are advancing—that is, they are covering more ground. But they are not growing or shrinking; they are simply getting thinner.[3]

Digging Into the Past

By drilling a hollow tube deep into the Antarctic ice sheet, scientists can pull out samples, called ice cores. The ice that they retrieve has been buried for hundreds of thousands of years. Like the rings of a very old tree, each layer of ice represents a particular point in time. The layers contain pockets of ancient air sealed in tiny bubbles with different concentrations of gases. Each layer contains information about the air quality and climate at the time.

A group of European scientists drilling on a high plateau on the East Antarctic Ice Sheet have extracted the deepest ice core yet, nearly two miles long. The very oldest layers of the core are 800,000 years old.[4]

The scientists can see past concentrations of carbon dioxide and methane—two of the main gases that cause global warming—in the slices. Each layer also

The Dry Valleys have cooled over the past few decades. But clues buried in the Antarctic ice reveal that the region has gradually become warmer over the last thousand years. Why do warmer global temperatures cause the Taylor Valley glaciers to advance, while the rest of the world's glaciers are shrinking? Fountain thinks he may have the answer.

Because the ice is so much colder in Antarctica than in other parts of the world, the ice is stiffer. Fountain used a computer model to see what would happen if the holds clues about the temperatures at the time the snow was deposited. By studying the entire length of the ice core, scientists learned that carbon dioxide levels and temperature rise and fall together. "Ice cores reveal the earth's natural climate rhythm over the last 800,000 years," said Eric Wolff, a glacier chemist with the British Antarctic Survey. "When carbon dioxide changed, there was always an accompanying climate change."[5]

The scientists found that the levels of carbon dioxide in the ice core had increased by about 35 percent in the past 200 years. This is roughly the time when humans began producing gases that influence the atmosphere. Before that time, the carbon dioxide levels were fairly steady. Not only are these levels in recent layers higher than ever, they are increasing at a far faster rate than before. This worries Wolff. "The ice core suggests that the increase in carbon dioxide will definitely give us a climate change that will be dangerous."[6]

temperature of the ice increased from -2.2°F (-19°C) to 1.4°F (-17°C). The warming temperatures cause the ice to soften a little. The model predicted that this would cause the glacier to spread out. This is exactly what Fountain has observed.[7]

Some glaciers in the coastal and lowland regions of the McMurdo Dry Valleys, on the other hand, have been shrinking fairly rapidly. Dirt on the glaciers causes them to absorb more heat from the sun. This has always been the case, but Fountain said that there has been more

An iceberg is a large piece of ice broken off from a glacier or ice shelf that floats in open water. About 90 percent of the iceberg is underwater.

sunlight in this region in the past decade—probably due to less cloud cover. "This is a climate warming-like signal," Fountain wrote. "Some of the changes we see today may mimic changes we see in the future when the climate of the region warms."[8]

Fountain has been fascinated with ice since he was in junior high, when a scientist came to his school to talk about making ice crystals. He was captivated. He soon taught himself how to collect snowflakes and preserve them on glass slides.

His interest in ice crystals continued when he went to college. He wanted to learn more about these tiny, jewel-like objects. One day, he was ice-skating on a lake in upstate New York. One of his companions pointed out the interesting bubble and crack patterns in the ice. Fountain soon realized that there was a whole world of ice-related research. He went to graduate school and studied snowflakes, river ice, lake ice, and sea ice.

After he earned his master's degree, he went to work for the United States Geological Survey (USGS). While there, he became so fascinated with glaciers that he earned his PhD studying them. He had never been really interested in glaciers before. They seemed too big and too hard to reach. Unlike delicate snowflakes, you could not hold them in your hand. But in 1993 Fountain was invited to study glaciers in Antarctica. He liked them. He has been studying them ever since, in Antarctica and around the world. He even has an Antarctic glacier named after him!

Inland Antarctica Cools as the World Warms: What Gives?

While the rest of the world is generally getting warmer, scientists have found that from 1986 to 2000, more than half of Antarctica was getting colder.[9] The rest of the continent, however, was getting warmer. What's the explanation? Scientists have a hypothesis.

Earth's rotation causes winds to circulate around the continent of Antarctica. The waters around Antarctica warm up, along with the rest of the world, but the frozen continent stays cold. As the temperature difference between the interior of the continent and the surrounding ocean increases, the winds go faster and faster. These winds do affect the Antarctic Peninsula, which is warming just like the rest of the world.

But the belt of winds circling the continent does not reach the Dry Valleys and other inland regions. Instead, it acts as a sort of fence, keeping the climate of the Dry Valleys and other inland regions isolated from the rest of the world.

This hypothesis explains why the main part of the continent is not becoming warmer. But why is it getting cooler? High in Earth's atmosphere is a level called the ozone layer. It acts like a blanket to trap the earth's heat. Human-made pollutants have destroyed a large part of the ozone layer over Antarctica. The hole in the ozone "blanket" may explain much of the continent's cooling. Now, the chemicals that destroy the ozone layer have been banned. As the ozone hole heals, the rest of the continent may warm up as well.

Fountain modestly said that Fountain Glacier is so insignificant that Robert Scott, who named most of the obvious glaciers in the area, "didn't even bother." He is happy about it, though, even though he has never actually set foot on "his" glacier. "It's kind of hard to get to," he said. "Sometimes when we're flying by on the helicopter, I look at it."

A researcher collects data as he overlooks Taylor Glacier.

Careers in Glaciology

Glaciologists are ice scientists who study glaciers. Their research relates to weather and climate change, to earth sciences and exploration, and to the history of Earth. Glaciologists often receive a college degree in a related science such as geology, physics, or chemistry, and then earn a master's or doctoral degree in glaciology. Many go on to gain postdoctoral research experience before entering the job market. They may find jobs at colleges or universities, with the government, or with petroleum and mining companies.

Glaciologists often work with professional mountaineers, who know how to navigate the ice safely. As global warming continues to heat the earth, melting glaciers could drastically affect ocean levels as well as local habitats. Glaciologists enjoy a mixture of office and research work, as well as fieldwork in cold, often harsh conditions. The median annual salary of geoscientists in 2013 was $108,420.[10]

Chapter 6

The Fingerprint of the Big Bang

Dr. Brian Keating goes to the South Pole to take baby pictures. Keating, an astrophysicist at the University of California, San Diego, doesn't take pictures of human babies. He helped build a telescope to peer back in time and take pictures of the baby universe—a mere trillionth of a trillionth of a trillionth of a second after it came into being.

Birth of the Universe

The most widely accepted theory about the beginning of the universe is the Big Bang model. This is the idea that our universe started out, nearly fourteen billion years ago, as an unimaginably hot, dense speck. When it exploded, all forms of matter and energy, as well as space and time itself, were formed. The universe expanded at incredible

Dr. Brian Keating takes a picture of his reflection in the shiny metal ball that sits at the South Pole.

speed. Almost as quickly as it began, the universe—now about ten feet (three meters) in diameter—put on the brakes. It continued to grow, much as a balloon expands when you blow it up, but at a slower pace.

For the next 400,000 years, the universe was a dense soup of particles and very high-energy light. Not the kind of light we can see with our eyes, but a kind of electromagnetic radiation called gamma rays. The light made it too hot for the particles to come together and form atoms. But the universe cooled as it continued to expand. Finally, it cooled enough for the particles to form atoms.

Today, fourteen billion years later, the universe continues to expand. As the universe cooled, the ultra-high-energy gamma rays stretched into X-rays, and then into visible light. Today, that first light has stretched all the way out to become microwaves.

Scientists have detected these ancient microwaves. They call them the cosmic microwave background (CMB). This radiation comes from every direction in the sky. Tiny differences in the energy, or temperature, of the CMB reveal certain areas that were slightly denser and hotter than other areas. These areas grew into stars and galaxies.

The discovery of the CMB allowed scientists to study the early universe. But the CMB only came into existence 400,000 years after the Big Bang. It is as though some unseen hand drew a curtain at that point. What

Waves of Energy

Electromagnetic radiation is the name that scientists give to energy that travels at the speed of light in wave-like patterns. When you listen to the radio, look at a sunset, or cook something in the microwave oven, you are using electromagnetic energy. The energy comes in bundles called photons.

At one end of the electromagnetic spectrum are radio waves. These are photons with low energies and long wavelengths. The wavelengths can be smaller than an inch or up to hundreds of miles long. Microwaves are shorter and more energetic. A microwave oven cooks food because microwaves cause water molecules in the food to rub up against each other and heat up. Next comes infrared radiation. We cannot see it, but we can feel it as heat. Visible light has wavelengths that our eyes can see. The sun and other stars give off ultraviolet light, the type of radiation that causes our skin to burn. Your doctor and dentist may use X-rays to look at your bones and teeth; they have very short wavelengths and high energy. Gamma rays have the shortest wavelength and highest energy of all radiation.

is behind the curtain? What did the universe look like during those first 400,000 years?

Keating and his colleagues hope that their new telescope will help them understand what happened behind that curtain. Scientists believe that the initial runaway expansion of the universe was so violent that it produced ripples in the fabric of space and time. If you throw a rock into the middle of a pond, the rock will create waves that move outward. The Big Bang acted like a huge rock, creating ripples in the universe. Scientists call these ripples gravitational waves.[1]

The gravitational waves would have been quite powerful in the moments following the Big Bang, just as a huge boulder thrown into the middle of a pond would create giant waves. But like the waves in the pond, the gravitational waves get weaker as they move outward. By the time they reach Earth, they are very difficult to detect.

Still, scientists believe that the Big Bang's gravitational waves should have left a faint fingerprint on the CMB. That is where Keating and his colleagues come in. They built a telescope, called BICEP (Background Imaging of Cosmic Extragalactic Polarization), designed to detect the gravitational waves' distinctive fingerprint.[2]

Keating and his colleagues spent years scanning the sky with BICEP. They built a faster and more sensitive version of the telescope, BICEP 2, and continued to search for the Big Bang's gravitational waves. Finally, in March 2014, the team of scientists announced that they detected a faint pattern of swirls that might well be the baby picture of the universe.

Keating is excited about the results, but in a TED talk he cautioned, "It may be that there are other explanations for these images…. It might be that microscopic grains of [space] dust…can get aligned by the weak magnetic fields in our galaxy, and form swirling patterns of microwaves which can masquerade as the pattern that we claim represents the genesis of the Big Bang."[3]

A Great Place to View Space

Why go to all the trouble of building a telescope at the South Pole? Simple: It is the very best place on Earth for astronomers to tune in to microwave signals.[4]

"Space is the best place, but space missions are very expensive," Keating says.[5] Water vapor in Earth's atmosphere absorbs microwaves, but because the South Pole is so high and cold, it is the driest place on Earth. It is even drier than the Sahara Desert! "We're going to a lot of trouble trying to detect this very faint radiation, producing only a billionth of a billionth of a watt of power, in our telescope," Keating explains. "We don't want water vapor to absorb a single photon."

Because the South Pole sits on Earth's axis of rotation, the same sky is visible all winter long. This allows scientists to focus the telescope on one patch of sky for a long period of time. And there are six months of near total darkness. This gives them a better chance of spotting the faint fingerprints of their elusive culprit.

Despite the possibility that their image of the universe is contaminated with space dust, Keating remains optimistic. He'll keep looking, using more and more sensitive instruments. "Imagine you're at a football stadium," he says, "with about a million people, and they're all chattering and making a lot of noise. But you

BICEP was designed to detect faint gravitational waves left over from the Big Bang—what scientists believe to be the beginning of the universe.

know that there is one person singing a pure note." With a lot of effort, he says, you could eventually detect the singer by recording the din of the stadium over a long period of time. By taking out the random noise of the crowd, eventually you would be left with the signal of that one single note. "We're looking for something that is ten to one hundred parts in a billion," Keating says.

Life at the South Pole Station

Keating flew to the South Pole to set up the telescopes. The flight from McMurdo Station to the South Pole took about three hours, on a plane that used skis instead of wheels for takeoff and landing. The difference between McMurdo Station and the South Pole, Keating said, is striking. "The coast is really beautiful and rugged, with glaciers and mountains." McMurdo is a busy place, "kind of like a cross between a mining town and a college campus."

The Amundsen-Scott South Pole Station, in contrast, sits atop a bare plateau of ice two miles thick. Keating and his colleagues lived in the South Pole Station, built on stilts to allow the snow to blow through. "It looks like a fortress from *Star Wars* or something," Keating said.

The station has dormitory rooms, a computer lab, a kitchen, and a dining room. There is even an entertainment room, with a TV and Ping-Pong and pool tables. "You get to meet people from all over the world," Keating said. "It's fun, and there's a lot of camaraderie, even though you are at the edge of the world. You still

A Giant Telescope

Keating and his BICEP colleagues are not the only astrophysicists doing research at the South Pole. In fact, you could say that the South Pole is a real hot spot for astrophysics.

In 2007, a group of scientists began looking at the sky through a new, giant telescope. Standing 75 feet (23 meters) tall and 33 feet (10 meters) across, and weighing 280 tons (254 metric tons), the South Pole Telescope (SPT) is also designed to detect CMB radiation. But the SPT scientists are not looking for the fingerprint of gravitational waves. They hope that the telescope will help them understand the nature of dark energy, a mysterious force that dominates the universe. Just as BICEP is looking for the fingerprints of gravitational waves left on the CMB, the South Pole Telescope will look for the signature of dark energy left on the CMB.

Astrophysicists believe that the universe has been expanding ever since the Big Bang. But in the late 1990s, astronomers found evidence that the expansion is speeding up. This led scientists to conclude that there is a force, called dark energy, pushing the universe apart. The SPT scientists are using the instrument to learn more about uncharted, far-flung clusters of galaxies. Because dark energy seems to push everything apart, studying the development of these clusters may reveal something about the nature of this mysterious force. "Everyone questions where we're coming from and how did this happen and what's out there," said John Carlstrom, the lead scientist for the project.[6]

feel like you are at the center of everything, because there are so many experiments there: physics, astronomy, atmospheric science, global warming studies—all sorts of things." There were dinner parties for the holidays, he said, with lobster, king crab, and steak. On December 25 there was even the annual Race Around the World, where people ran around the pole. This 2.5-mile (4-km) race took them through all of the world's time zones.

But Keating, like everyone else at the South Pole Station, also worked hard. Every day, he walked out

BICEP is housed in a building called the Dark Sector Laboratory, center. The South Pole Telescope is on the left.

An American flag is displayed at the South Pole Station. The South Pole attracts scientists from around the world for its unique position and environment.

to the observatory housing the telescope, about three-quarters of a mile (one kilometer) across the runway. At first, he said, he ran out of breath very easily because the atmosphere is so thin. Not only is the station sitting atop 2 miles (3 km) of ice, but also Earth's rotation thins the atmosphere even more. This makes it feel even higher. He spent much of his time installing the telescope and other instruments in the tower of the observatory.

After his first trip to Antarctica, Keating wrote in his blog, "All in all, an amazing, life-altering trip. Looking forward to my next trip."[7]

Careers in Astrophysics

An astrophysicist uses physics to study the nature and behavior of our universe. These days, the words astronomy and astrophysics mean pretty much the same thing. The popular image of the astronomer is someone who looks at stars and constellations through a telescope. But that almost never happens anymore. Although many (but not all) astrophysicists use telescopes to study the universe, the tools used to gather and analyze the data are so sophisticated that it is often not possible for a human eye to look through them.

If you would like to become an astrophysicist, you should take as many courses in math and science as you can. Most astrophysicists earn a degree in physics or astronomy in college. To be a research astrophysicist or professor, you will need to earn a PhD in either physics or astronomy, depending on the university. Most astrophysicists then spend two to six years in a temporary position as a postdoctoral scholar before finding a permanent job.

Many astrophysicists find jobs in research universities or colleges. Some are employed by private industry, making telescopes or writing specialized computer software. Others work at government-funded observatories and research centers. The National Aeronautics and Space Administration (NASA) employs many astrophysicists. There is a growing number of jobs open to astrophysicists at science museums and planetariums. The median annual earnings of physicists and astronomers were $117,040 in 2013.[8]

Chapter 7

Athletes Under the Ice

People who encounter a Weddell seal for the first time on land might be excused if they don't immediately recognize it as a supreme athlete. The Weddell seal, which makes its home on the coast and in the waters of Antarctica, is really cute. Its whiskered mouth and large round eyes might remind you of a contented cat. It is not afraid of humans, so you might well be able to stroke the rolls of fat folding down its neck as it raises its head to greet you. But do not let its appearance fool you. In the waters under Antarctica's coastal ice, Weddell seals are among the most elite athletes of the animal world.

An adult Weddell seal can dive under the ice in the frigid waters of the Southern Ocean for more than an hour at a time. It stalks and hunts fish, squid, even the occasional octopus. It dives to depths that would crush the lungs of a human diver—all while holding its breath! How does it do it? That is what Dr. Shane Kanatous, a physiology professor at Colorado State University, would like to know. His goal is to apply the secrets of diving mammals to medicine. He hopes that his research will help patients who are recovering from heart attacks and surgery.

The Seals of Muscle Beach

You have probably noticed that you breathe faster and your heart beats more quickly when you exercise. This is your body's attempt to get more oxygen to your muscles, where it is needed. But Weddell seals and other marine mammals must hold their breath for long periods of time while exercising. One of the seals' secrets to their amazing abilities is myoglobin. Myoglobin is a protein found in the muscles that power the heart and movement. It binds with oxygen to keep oxygen in the muscle.[1] Kanatous and his team wanted to know how myoglobin levels change over a seal's lifetime, and what causes that change.

Kanatous made his fifth trip to Antarctica in late 2006 to study the seals. For more than eight weeks, he and his team members lived at McMurdo Station. Each day, they traveled to a field site they nicknamed "Muscle Beach." They picked the site because it is near ice cracks where the seals normally gather when they are not in the water.

Weddell seals are able to dive deep underwater for over an hour at a time.

There, they set up a place to keep out of the cold when they were not working with the seals. Their one-room orange hut was not much, but it did provide some shelter from the elements. "It gets a little bit cold," admitted Kanatous. "Winds can range anywhere from dead calm to in excess of 40 miles [64 kilometers] per hour."[2] Each day, weather permitting, they took snowmobiles and a specially equipped truck to Muscle Beach. The truck had tracks that allowed it to travel on the sea ice instead of wheels.

There, they looked for seals hauled out on the ice. Because the team was interested in learning how the seals' muscles change as they get older, they studied three- to four-week-old pups, before the pups learned to dive. They also studied juveniles (teenagers, at one to two years of age) as well as adults. The juveniles tend to be solitary and difficult to find, Kanatous said. Adult males guard their territories (and breathing holes) jealously. It is difficult for a small juvenile to get past the larger males. They must venture farther away to find their own breathing holes and hunting territories.

Adult Weddell seals can grow to be 3 meters (10 feet) long and weigh over 1,000 pounds (450 kilograms), but because they have no natural predators, they are amazingly gentle. "They're very powerful animals," Kanatous said. "Their bodies are mostly muscle from the neck down. They have no idea they can severely injure you."

Dr. Shane Kanatous is a physiology professor and marine biologist who studies the Weddell seals of Antarctica.

Once they located a suitable animal, the scientists herded it away from the other animals. They put a leather bag over the seal's head to calm it, and gave it a sedative. They weighed the animal, used an ultrasound machine to determine how much blubber it had, and took its temperature. Finally, they took small muscle samples from different parts of the seal's body. As far as the seals were concerned, the sampling needle would feel like a mosquito bite, Kanatous said. The whole process took about thirty minutes. They put the muscle samples in a special solution, so that they could be analyzed later in the laboratory.

When they examined the muscles of seal pups, Kanatous and his team were surprised to learn that the pups already had ten times more myoglobin in their muscles than did land-based animals at birth. The pups had not even begun to dive, so they did not need such high levels of myoglobin. Kanatous explained that this was probably because their mothers were diving all the time while they were carrying their unborn pups. Even before the pups were born, their muscles were receiving signals to make more myoglobin.

A Weddell seal mother with her very young pup. These seals live farther south than any other mammal.

Juveniles have the highest levels of myoglobin. Because they cannot dive as deeply as adults, they have to make up for it by swimming faster, for shorter periods of time. They work harder underwater than adults, so they need to store more oxygen in their muscles.

Kanatous and his colleagues grew the Weddell muscle cells in the laboratory—the first laboratory in the world to grow and maintain the muscle cells from diving animals. That was a big accomplishment—and not easy to do! There is a good reason to study these remarkable cells: If they can determine what triggers cells to make more myoglobin, their research could benefit human patients recovering from heart attacks and heart surgery.[3]

"If we knew how to increase myoglobin in the heart of a patient before open-heart surgery, we could give that person a better chance of recovery," Kanatous says. "In addition, if we could increase myoglobin in the skeletal muscles of people with heart disease, they could exercise better."

Now they are working to repeat their success with the muscle cells of Weddell seals with those of a species a little closer to home: elephant seals.

One of the really interesting things about the muscle cells of elephant seals, Kanatous said, are their mitochondria—the power stations of cells. Their mitochondria is different from that of most mammals because they are really good at generating lots of heat AND energy at the same time.

Kanatous plans to return to Antarctica soon to study the effects of climate change on the seals. "These animals dive on an oxygen budget," he says. "Anything that makes them use more oxygen is going to shorten their dives."

Body fat is an important stored energy source for the seals—and for people, too. There are different kinds of fats—think of the difference between butterfat and peanut butter. Most of the fat in the seals' bodies resembles the fat in peanut butter. It requires little oxygen to be turned into energy. But scientists who study fish

Kanatous and other researchers are now working with the cells of elephant seals in their efforts to help heart patients.

A Weddell seal swims in the icy waters of Antarctica. Scientists are concerned about the effects of global warming on the seals and their ability to store oxygen.

have found that when water temperature increases, the makeup of their body fat changes. These new types of fats require more oxygen to be turned into energy.

If warming ocean temperatures cause the Weddell seals to develop more of these new fats, it could mean that they have less time to hunt under the ice—and less food to eat.

"If we knew how to increase myoglobin in the heart of a patient before open-heart surgery, we could give that person a better chance of recovery," Kanatous says. "In addition, if we could increase myoglobin in the skeletal muscles of people with heart disease, they could exercise better."

The Secrets of Frosty Fish

Antarctic waters are so cold that most fish would soon freeze in the chilly depths. The presence of salt in seawater allows it to remain liquid until about 28°F (−2°C), well below the freezing point of freshwater. But the blood of Antarctic fish is only about one-half as salty as seawater. They need something else to prevent their blood from freezing. What they have are glycoproteins (proteins with sugar attached). These proteins act as antifreeze.

Arthur DeVries, a professor of biology at the University of Illinois, discovered these antifreeze proteins in a giant Antarctic cod in 1971. The proteins circulate in the blood of the fish. They bind to tiny ice crystals and prevent them from growing larger. But for decades scientists did not know how or where the fish made these special compounds. Finally, in 2006,

The Making of a Marine Biologist

Kanatous, who grew up in New York City, became fascinated by marine life and the ocean at a very young age. He was a big fan of Jacques Cousteau, the French oceanographer who introduced the undersea world to millions of people through his popular television series and books. Kanatous's parents, who were originally from Puerto Rico and Lebanon, were "extraordinarily supportive," he says. "That was fortunate for me, because

Chi-Hing Christina Cheng, a professor of biology at the University of Illinois and a colleague of DeVries, solved the mystery.

"Ever since the discovery of these antifreeze proteins, it was assumed that they had to be produced in the liver," Cheng said.[4] She explained that most animals made blood proteins in the liver. Instead, the antifreeze proteins are made in the pancreas, an organ that normally makes digestive enzymes, and in the stomach.[5]

That is not the only surprising thing Cheng learned about these proteins. She found that the antifreeze protein evolved in the fish when Earth began its dramatic cooling trend. The once-mild waters surrounding Antarctica turned icy. The fish had to adapt, or die.

Surprisingly, Cheng found that these antifreeze proteins also prevent the ice crystals from melting when the fish swim in warmer waters. So the antifreeze proteins are also, Cheng says, "anti-melt proteins as well."[6]

I didn't know many people in New York City who wanted to be marine biologists!"

During his senior year in high school, he met the director of the New York Aquarium, who encouraged him to study marine science at Southampton College of Long Island. The turning point, he said, came in his senior year at Southampton College. He had the good fortune to work as an intern in the laboratory of Gerald Kooyman. Kooyman was one of the leading experts on diving mammals and birds at the Scripps Institution

Careers in Marine Biology

Marine biology is the scientific study of the plants, animals, and microbes that live in the oceans and on their shorelines. Because there are so many topics that a marine biologist could study, most researchers specialize in a particular area of interest. They may choose to learn everything they can about a certain species of clam, for instance. They may study the unique ecosystem surrounding deep-sea volcanoes. Or they may focus on the way pollution affects marine life near heavily populated areas. Like Kanatous, they may study the physiology of marine animals to learn how they adapt to their environment.

One area of specialization, marine biotechnology, offers great opportunity for marine biologists. Marine biotechnologists may test and develop drugs that come from marine organisms, for example.

Field research on research ships at sea or in other far-flung spots is a job requirement for many marine biologists. Most also spend a fair amount of time doing

of Oceanography at the University of California–San Diego. During that year, they studied California sea lions, harbor seals, penguins, and thick-billed murres (another diving bird).

"I have always wanted to know why things work the way they do," Kanatous says. "I was very fortunate to find a field that I just love, physiology; and I can use diving mammals as one of the models I work with."

laboratory research, writing papers and grant proposals, and analyzing data.

If you want to be a marine biologist, you should study marine biology or a related area such as biochemistry, biology, ecology, botany, microbiology, or zoology in college. People with college degrees can often get jobs as research assistants. Most research positions require at least a master's degree, but preferably a PhD, in marine science. Many marine biologists, especially those wishing to become professors, will take temporary postdoctoral positions before they find a permanent job.

Marine biologists may find research and teaching positions at colleges or universities. Many marine biologists find work at government laboratories or with state fishery or environmental agencies. They may work for private companies that need the expertise of a marine biologist or for an aquarium or zoo. Salaries for marine biologists depend on their specialties. The median annual earnings of wildlife biologists and zoologists was $62,610 in 2013.[7]

Kanatous is sure to return to Antarctica. "There are a lot of interesting questions about how these animals are adapted to their environment," he says. He wants to learn how newborn seal pups survive in the extreme cold, for example. "With most research, when you open a door and start to find answers, you find five more doors in front of you that need to be opened."

Chapter 8

Climate Clues to Ice Melt

In early 2002, Dr. Eugene Domack took a research cruise to the Antarctic Peninsula. Domack, a professor of Earth science at the University of South Florida, studies the mud on the ocean floor near Antarctica to learn how the climate has changed over the past hundreds of thousands of years.

It was the warmest summer on record for the peninsula. One especially fine January day, they sailed into the Weddell Sea, near a large ice shelf called Larsen B. Ice shelves are huge expanses of floating ice attached to the ice sheets that cover the Antarctic continent. This ice shelf was about the size of the state of Rhode Island.

"There was not a breeze, the water was like glass, and the temperature was in the forties [Fahrenheit]," Domack said. Incredibly, he and his shipmates saw a

Dr. Eugene Domack, pictured here in Namibia, studies mud from the Antarctic ocean floor to determine how the continent's climate has changed over hundreds of years.

chain of waterfalls cascading off the ice shelf. "No one, and there were a lot of experienced people on that ship, had ever seen anything like it. The water in front of the glacier was brown, murky with mud."[1]

Domack and his team collected six sediment cores from the area. Two months later, the Larsen B ice shelf collapsed. Seven hundred twenty billion tons (653 billion metric tons) of ice—enough for twelve trillion big bags of party ice—splintered into drifting icebergs.

What had caused the dramatic breakup of the ice shelf? Was it a result of Earth's normal warming and cooling cycles? Was the ice shelf a victim of an unstable base, or were unusually warm air temperatures the culprit? The Antarctic Peninsula has warmed by about 4°F (2°C) in the past fifty years.

Domack returned to the Peninsula in 2005, collecting more core samples, this time from the seabed that had once been covered by the collapsed ice shelf.

When Domack analyzed his core samples, he found that the Larsen B ice shelf had been firmly in place for at least 11,000 years, despite normal climate variations.[2] The evidence shows that while the ice shelf had thinned somewhat over thousands of years, it must have been this recent surge in temperature that caused the collapse of Larsen B. What's more, he was able to show that the warming air, and not an unstable base, was responsible for the collapse of the ice shelf.[3]

The collapse of the Larsen B ice shelf is part of an alarming trend. The ice shelves appear to hold back the

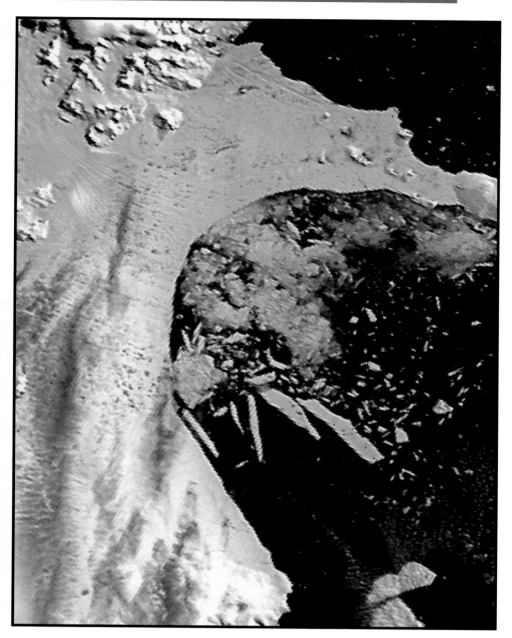

An instrument called a Moderate Resolution Imaging Spectroradiometer (MODIS) on a NASA satellite recorded the 2002 collapse of the Larsen B ice shelf. Glaciologists are concerned about all the ice shelves on the Antarctic Peninsula.

massive glaciers that make up Antarctica's ice sheets. As those ice shelves continue to melt, the entire West Antarctic ice sheet is beginning to collapse. It won't happen right away—scientists say that the collapse will take 200 to 1,000 years—but it does appear that there is nothing we can do to stop it. The sheet contains enough ice to raise the Earth's ocean level by 4 feet (1.2 meters), which would be a disaster for many islands and coastal areas.[4]

Climate History in the Mud

The mud on the seafloor off the coast of Antarctica tells a story that goes back thousands of years. The trick is learning to read the language in which it is written. When living things in the ocean die, they sink to the bottom, forming a fossil layer. Most of these are one-celled organisms such as algae. When the climate warms, the coastal glaciers slowly begin to melt. Meltwater flows into the ocean, bringing with it sand and clay.

Domack and his team of researchers pull out long, cylinder-shaped samples of mud, similar to ice core samples, from the ocean floor. They use a winch and steel cable to lower the core sampler to the ocean floor. It takes hours of hard work to pull up a single sample of mud.

Inside the ship's laboratory, the scientists cut the cylinder into thin slices. They photograph each slice and examine its contents carefully. Each sample has alternating layers of biological material and mud from the glaciers. They determine the age of each layer using radiocarbon dating.

When the scientists put all the information together, the layers tell the story of natural warming and cooling cycles over thousands of years. When the climate becomes warmer, meltwater from the ice shelves carries sand and clay into the ocean. This mud sinks to the bottom, mixing in with the remains of dead organisms. The layers with lots of mud mixed in with the biological material indicate a warm period. When the climate is cooler, there is less meltwater (and mud) from the ice shelves. The layers from these periods are rich in biological material, with less mud. These cycles, Domack says, are caused by changes in the energy output of the sun.

Death of an Ecosystem

When Domack and his team returned to the site of the collapsed Larsen B ice shelf in 2005, they used an underwater video camera to film the deepest part of the basin. It was more than 2,000 feet (610 meters) below the surface. They did not get around to watching the videotape until they were already headed back to port. But when did, they were amazed. "The bottom looked kind of weird—all white and bumpy," Domack said. "It didn't look like anything I'd seen before."

The white stuff turned out to be a type of bacteria, called *Beggiatoa*. These bacteria, which grow in a blanket-like mat, get their energy from chemicals rather than the sun. On top of the mat were clusters of giant

Earth's Global Conveyer Belt

Antarctica may seem to be an isolated part of the world, but Antarctica's Southern Ocean has a huge effect on all of us. It is the only ocean that circles the globe without being blocked by land. Its current flow, the Antarctic Circumpolar Current, has a powerful influence on Earth's climate. The current surrounding Antarctica is 13,049 miles (21,000 kilometers) long, and transports 34 billion gallons (130 billion liters) of water each second. That is 150 times the flow of all Earth's rivers put together![5]

The Antarctic Circumpolar Current connects the Indian, Atlantic, and Pacific Ocean basins. It is a huge conveyor belt that circulates water, heat, and chemicals from one part of the world to another. As water enters the polar regions, it gets colder. Some of it freezes, causing the remaining water to become saltier. The extra-salty water is denser, so it sinks from the surface into the deep ocean. Lighter, warmer water flows in to replace the sinking water. The temperature and salt differences are like the motor driving the conveyor belt. The heat transferred from the equator to the poles by

clams. The team had found a cold seep, a place where underwater mud volcanoes spew out chemicals such as methane and hydrogen sulfide. It was an ecosystem that had been isolated under a thick cap of ice for 10,000 years, until the collapse of the ice shelf.

the ocean's currents influences temperature and rainfall all over the world.

Janet Sprintall is a physical oceanographer at the Scripps Institution of Oceanography, San Diego. She studies ocean currents in the Drake Passage, located between the northernmost tip of the Antarctic Peninsula and the southernmost tip of South America. This is the narrowest point for the current to pass through, so it gives scientists a great location to study this global conveyor belt. Sprintall collects data on temperature and saline levels in the Drake Passage by launching probes off the deck of research vessels into the passage.

Scientists are concerned that global warming may cause the conveyor belt to slow dramatically. Two of the effects of global warming would be increased rainfall and melting ice near the poles. This would increase the amount of freshwater in those places. Remember that freshwater is not as dense as saltwater. If too much freshwater is added to the ocean current, then no matter how cold the water becomes, it will not sink. The motor that drives the conveyor belt would slow or even stop. If that happens, Western Europe and the eastern part of North America would cool dramatically, even as the rest of the world gets warmer.

Scientists have found similar cold-seep ecosystems in other parts of the ocean, but never in such a cold, extreme environment. It was definitely the biggest thing Domack had been involved with in the Antarctic. By the time they knew what they had found, he said, it was too late to return to take samples. All they had was the video.

In 2007 scientists on a German research vessel returned to the area as part of a larger effort to learn more about Antarctic marine life. They found the site, Domack said, but everything was dead. "The system is being buried," he said. Buried, that is, as the icebergs melt and dump all of their sediment onto the seafloor. "All you can see are a few clams sticking up above the seafloor," he continued, "but the shells are open and they're dead."

Domack hypothesizes that the ice shelf acted like a protective lid over the ecosystem. The ecosystem existed *because* of the ice shelf, not in spite of it.

Scientists are now convinced that the recent warming trend is caused in large part by pollution in the atmosphere.[6] Domack said that these changes are an indication of just how much human activities affect the planet. "Our reach has gone not just to Antarctica, but to this deep trough in the most restricted, remote place, to a deep cavity at the bottom of the ocean. If human activity has reached that far, then we are having a big impact; we need to think about this, and maybe we need to change."[7]

Oceanographers can find jobs as teachers or researchers in colleges and universities. Government laboratories and private industries employ many oceanographers. Oceanography is a geoscience, and the median yearly pay for geoscientists in 2013 was $108,420.[8]

Careers in Oceanography

Oceanography is the scientific study of the oceans and the way they work. Oceanographers are likely to specialize in one of four main areas.

- *Physical oceanographers* study the circulation of the ocean, its influence on biological and chemical processes, and the interaction of the ocean with the atmosphere.

- *Chemical oceanographers* study natural and human-made chemicals in the ocean and on the seafloor.

- *Geological oceanographers* study the seafloor: its shape, the nature of its sediments, and the crust beneath. They may specialize in studying and predicting geological events, such as underwater volcanic action or earthquakes.

- *Biological oceanographers* study the complex interactions between marine organisms and their environment.

To become an oceanographer, take plenty of math and science courses in high school. A college degree in biology, mathematics, physics, chemistry, or geology is good preparation for a career in oceanography. Most research positions require a master's or doctoral degree. Those with doctoral degrees often carry out additional research before finding permanent positions.

Oceanographers often travel around the world as part of their research, living and working on research vessels. But like scientists in many other fields, they spend most of their time analyzing and interpreting data in the laboratory.

Rough Water on the Drake Passage

Domack has been digging for answers about past Antarctic climates for many years. In 1978, he joined a research cruise near Wilkes Land, "an often ignored little corner of the world on the east Antarctic margin," Domack said. He was a young graduate student, and this was his first time out of the United States. Domack worked twelve-hour shifts, in weather that sometimes dipped to −50°F (−45°C), and loved every minute. "I just thought, this is it for me. I had to come back and find out what this place is all about. I was hooked."

Domack has been the chief scientist on many research cruises. His 2006 cruise began in Punta Arenas, Chile, where he boarded the *Nathaniel B. Palmer*, one of the specially equipped research ships operated by the United States Antarctic Program. In addition to the support crew, the science crew included marine geologists, sedimentologists, oceanographers, paleontologists, and students.

To reach Antarctica, the ships had to cross the Drake Passage, infamous for its rough waters. In his 2006 expedition blog, Domack wrote, "We had our first taste of the real Drake Passage during the last 24 hours. Most students are down for a while as the seas have been rough. While the *Palmer* is a steady vessel, we did take some rolls and pitches that sent students from the watch stand to the bunk."[9]

The crew worked hard, mapping and collecting data about the seafloor. The 2006 trip was especially

The Drake Passage lies between the southern tip of South America and Antarctica. It is known for its rough waters.

Researchers who visit Antarctica encounter harsh working conditions and freezing temperatures, but they also experience the unique beauty of an area that few people have the chance to see.

challenging because it took place in late fall, just before the start of the polar winter. More and more pack ice began to fill the Weddell Sea, making the journey home slow going.

That year, Domack wrote in his blog:

April 28th brings us just off Robertson Island and the long three-day battle against the Weddell Sea pack ice has begun to show progress. Robertson Island was the locale that Sir Ernest Shackleton and his crew of the Endurance *were aiming for while they drifted and edged across the pack ice of the Weddell Sea in 1915. It now rises off our port side as an impressive dome of ice, with a bit of dark rock along its southern tip. The island serves as the doorway to entering and leaving the southern waters of this region. Since it sits so far east of the mainland, pack ice can alternatively wedge up against it (shutting the door) or blow out away to the east (opening the door). The ice is most definitely hard up against the island now, so the* Palmer *has to break down the door if we are to make our way north. We are almost through.*[10]

Life on a research ship can be challenging. "But I've been doing this for over twenty years, and I've taken over a hundred students with me," Domack said. "I'm very proud that no one on my cruise has so much as cut a finger. We do it really safely."

No matter how many times Domack visits Antarctica, the beauty of the place always amazes him. He remembers a quiet moment on the 2005 cruise: "You stand on the deck with whoever you're working with, and you see the sun coming up. There's this brilliant orange glow up over the mountains and the glaciers, and you see the tops of the icebergs slowly breaking the horizon as it becomes more lit. To be there as someone who is uncovering the secrets of the place is just a tremendously gratifying and humbling experience. To realize that you do this for a living—wow!"

Antarctica can seem far removed from our everyday lives. Scientists know that is far from the truth. Climate change is forcing the rest of the world to look to our coldest, driest, and most remote continent. NASA scientists have concluded that water eating away at the Antarctic ice has melted 130 billion tons (118 billion metric tons) of ice each year for the past decade—enough ice to fill more than 1.3 million Olympic swimming pools.[11] As the situation worsens, coastal areas around the globe are threatened. Scientists who study the earth's polar regions are working to discover the causes for this climate change and what can be done about it. It's clear that the world's fate hangs on the question of Antarctica's melting ice.

Appendix: Polar Scientists: Jobs at a Glance[1]

PALEONTOLOGIST	
Education Required	Bachelor of science degree in geology and/or biology; master's degree or, preferably, PhD and postdoctoral research in paleontology
Average Salary*	$108,420
GEOLOGIST	
Education Required	Bachelor of science degree in geology or earth science; master's degree in geology; PhD and postdoctoral research for teaching or high-level research position
Average Salary	$108,420
ECOLOGIST	
Education Required	Bachelor of science degree in biology, ecology, geology, environmental science, chemistry, or climatology; master's degree; PhD and postdoctoral research for teaching or high-level research position
Average Salary	$70,770
GLACIOLOGIST	
Education Required	Bachelor of science degree in geology, physics, or chemistry; master's degree in glaciology; PhD and postdoctoral research for teaching or high-level research position
Average Salary	$108,420
ASTROPHYSICIST	
Education Required	Bachelor of science degree in physics or astronomy; PhD in physics or astronomy; two to six years as postdoctoral scholar is common
Average Salary	$117,040
MARINE BIOLOGIST	
Education Required	Bachelor of science degree in marine biology, biology, biochemistry, ecology, botany, microbiology, or zoology; master's degree or, preferably, PhD in marine science for research position
Average Salary	$62,610
OCEANOGRAPHER	
Education Required	Bachelor of science degree in biology, mathematics, physics, chemistry, or biology; master's degree or, preferably, PhD for research position
Average Salary	$108,420

[1] Bureau of Labor Statistics, *Occupational Outlook Handbook, 2014–15 Edition,* May 2013, US Department of Labor, http://www.bls.gov/oes/current/oes_stru.htm.

*Salary figures will vary according to job specifications, geographic location, and market demands.

Chapter Notes

Chapter 1. This Laboratory Is Freezing!

1. Bernard Stonehouse, ed., *Encyclopedia of Antarctica and the Southern Oceans* (New York: John Wiley & Sons, 2002), 76.

2. Frederick Albert Cook, *Through the First Antarctic Night, 1898–1899: A Narrative of the Voyage of the "Belgica" Among Newly Discovered Lands and Over an Unknown Sea About the South Pole* (New York: Doubleday & McClure, 1900), 231.

3. Charles Turley, *The Voyages of Captain Scott* (Whitefish, Mont.: Kessinger, 2004), 247.

4. Lisa Mastro and Jim Mastro, "Life in Antarctica," *Antarctica Online*, accessed February 13, 2015, <http://www.antarcticaonline.com/culture/culture.htm>.

Chapter 2. Dinosaurs Frozen in Time

1. William R. Hammer, "Jurassic Dinosaurs from Antarctica," *Dinofest™ International Proceedings* (1997), 249–251.

2. William Hammer, personal interview, November 14, 2006. Unless otherwise indicated, all quotes from Hammer come from this interview.

3. Bureau of Labor Statistics, US Department of Labor, *Occupational Outlook Handbook, 2014-15 Edition*, Geoscientists, <http://www.bls.gov/oes/current/oes192042.htm>.

4. John Pickrell, "Two New Dinosaurs Discovered in Antarctica," *National Geographic News*, March 9, 2004, <http://www.news.nationalgeographic.com/news/2004/03/0309_040309_polardinos_2.html>.

5. Peter West, "Evidence of a 'Lost World': Antarctica Yields Two Unknown Dinosaur Species," National Science

Foundation press release, February 26, 2004, <http://www.nsf.gov/news/news_summ.jsp?cntn_id= 100340>.

6. Peter West, "Digging Dinosaurs—How Scientists Put the Pieces Together," National Science Foundation Fact Sheet, February 1, 2004, <http://www.nsf.gov/news/ news_summ.jsp?cntn_id=100606>.

Chapter 3. Space Rocks (on Earth)

1. Ralph Harvey, personal interview, November 7, 2006. Unless otherwise indicated, all quotes from Harvey come from this interview.

2. R.R. Frese, L. Potts et. al., "Permian-Triassic mascon in Antarctica," *Eos Trans. AGU, Jt. Assem. Suppl.* Vol 87, 36, Abstract T41A-08, 2006.

3. Ralph Harvey, *ANSMET Dispatches*, accessed February 13, 2015, <http://www.humanedgetech.com/expedition/ansmet/showDispatch.php?id=22541>.

4. Bureau of Labor Statistics, US Department of Labor, *Occupational Outlook Handbook, 2014-15 Edition*, Geoscientists, <http://www.bls.gov/oes/current/oes192042.htm>.

5. *Antarctic Meteorite Newsletter* 30, no. 1 (February 2007), <http://curator.jsc.nasa.gov/antmet/amn/amnfeb07/ProgramNews.htm>.

6. Jet Propulsion Laboratory, California Institute of Technology, *Mars Meteorite Homepage*, accessed February 13, 2015, <http:// www2.jpl.nasa.gov/snc/index.html>.

7. Emily Stone, "Antarctic Meteorites: Chip Off the Red Planet," *The Antarctic Sun*, October 30, 2004, <http://antarcticsun.usap.gov/oldissues2004-2005/ Sun102404/index.htm>.

Chapter 4. A Big Job for Tiny Worms

1. Robert Falcon Scott, *The Voyage of the Discovery,* Vol. II (London: MacMillan, 1905).

2. Edward O. Wilson, *The Future of Life* (New York: Knopf, 2002), 3–4.

3. Diana Wall, personal interview, November 28, 2006. Unless otherwise indicated, all quotes from Wall come from this interview.

4. Peter T. Doran et. al., "Formation and Character of an Ancient 19-m Ice Cover and Underlying Trapped Brine in an 'Ice-sealed' East Antarctic Lake," *Proceedings of the National Academy of Sciences* 100, No. 1, January 7, 2003, 26–31.

5. "Researchers Uncover Extreme Lake—and 3000-Year-Old Microbes—in Mars-like Antarctic Environment," National Science Foundation, Office of Legislative and Public Affairs news release, accessed February 13, 2015, <http://www.nsf.gov/od/lpa/news/ 02/pr02100.htm>.

6. Evelyn Boswell, "U.S. Expedition Yields First Breakthrough Paper about lLfe under Antarctic Ice," University Communications, Montana State University, accessed February 1, 2014, <http://www.montana.edu/news/15002/ u-s-expedition-yields-first-breakthrough-paper-about-life-under-antarctic-ice>.

7. Jane O'Brian, "Antarctic Nematodes and Climate Change," *BBC News*, April 26, 2013, <http://www.bbc.com/news/ magazine-22177221>.

8. Bureau of Labor Statistics, US Department of Labor, *Occupational Outlook Handbook, 2014–15 Edition*, Environmental Scientists and Specialists, <http://www.bls.gov/oes/current/oes192041.htm>.

9. "Antarctic Nnematodes and Climate Change," *BBC News*, April 26, 2013, accessed January 29, 2015, <http://www.bbc.com/news/magazine-22177221>.

10. Amanda Leigh Haag, "An Antarctic Ecosystem Shows Signs of Trouble as a Tiny Worm Turns," *New York Times*, November 21, 2006, D3.

11. "Polar Discoveries. Slide Show: Dry Valley Organisms," *PBS Online NewsHour*, February 23, 2007, <http://www.pbs.org/newshour/indepth_coverage/science/poles/slideshow_audio/index_flash.html>.

Chapter 5. Secrets of the Glaciers

1. Personal interview, Andrew Fountain, December 6, 2006. Unless otherwise indicated, all quotes from Fountain come from this interview.

2. Nathan Giles, "Andrew Fountain Examines the Inner Workings of Glaciers," AAAS Member Spotlight, December 17, 2014, accessed January 30, 2015, <http://membercentral.aaas.org/blogs/member-spotlight/andrew-fountain-examines-inner-workings-glaciers>.

3. Andrew G. Fountain et. al., "Glacier Mass Balances (1993–2001), Taylor Valley, McMurdo Dry Valleys, Antarctica," *Journal of Glaciology* 52, No. 178, 2006, 451–462.

4. Eric W. Wolff, "Understanding the Past: Climate History from Antarctica," *Antarctic Science*, 17, 2005, 487–495.

5. Jonathon Amos, "Deep Ice Tells Long Climate Story," *BBC News*, September 4, 2006, <http:// news.bbc.co.uk/2/hi/science/nature/5314592.stm>.

6. Ibid.

7. Andrew Fountain et. al., "Can Climate Warming Induce Glacier Advance in Taylor Valley, Antarctica?" *Journal of Glaciology* 50, No. 171, 2004, 556–564.

8. Andrew Fountain et. al., "The McMurdo Dry Valleys: A Landscape on the Threshold of Change," *Geomorphology* 225, November 14, 2014, 25–35; and personal email communication.

9. Peter T. Doran et. al., "Antarctic Climate Cooling and Terrestrial Ecosystem Response," *Nature* 415, January 31, 2002, 517–520.

10. Bureau of Labor Statistics, US Department of Labor, *Occupational Outlook Handbook, 2014–15 Edition*, Geoscientists, <http://www.bls.gov/oes/current/oes192042.htm>.

Chapter 6. The Fingerprint of the Big Bang

1. Brian G. Keating et. al., "The Polarization of the Cosmic Microwave Background Due to Primordial Gravitational Waves," *International Journal of Modern Physics*, A21, 2006, 2459–2479.

2. K.W. Yoon et. al., "The Robinson Gravitational Wave Background Telescope (BICEP): A Biometric Large Angulae Scale CMB Polarimeter," *Millimeter and Submillimeter Detectors and Instrumentation for Astronomy III, Proceedings of SPIE*, 6275, 2006.

3. Brian Keating, "Going to the Ends of the Earth to Discover the Beginning of Time," TEDxSanDiego, January 2, 2015, <https://www.youtube.com/watch?v=T22s4jCZ4Ho>.

4. Daniel Clery, "For Extreme Astronomy, Head Due South," *Science* 315, March 16, 2007, 1523–1524.

5. Personal interview, Brian Keating, November 13, 2006. Unless otherwise indicated, all quotes from Keating come from this interview.

6. Steve Martaindale, "Scientists Seek Big Discoveries with New Tool," *Antarctic Sun*, January 21, 2007, 11, <http://antarcticsun.usap.gov/>.

7. Bricep—My Trip to the South Pole, January 9, 2006, http://bricep.blogspot.com/.

8. Bureau of Labor Statistics, US Department of Labor, *Occupational Outlook Handbook, 2014–15 Edition*, Physicists and Astronomers, <http://www.bls.gov/oes/current/oes192012.htm>.

Chapter 7. Athletes Under the Ice

1. T.J. Wright and R.W. Davis, "The Effect of Myoglobin Concentration on Aerobic Dive Limit in a Weddell Seal," *Journal of Experimental Biology*, 209, Pt. 13, July 2006, 2576-2585.

2. Personal interviews, Shane Kanatous, December 22, 2006, and February 6, 2015. Unless otherwise indicated, all quotes from Kanatous come from these interviews.

3. D.J. Garry, S.B. Kanatous, and P.P. Mammen, "Emerging Roles for Myoglobin in the Heart," *Trends in Cardiovascular Medicine* 13, April 2003, 111–116.

4. "Researchers Discover Which Organs in Antarctic Fish Produce Antifreeze," *Science Daily*, June 28, 2006, <http://www.sciencedaily.com/releases/2006/06/060628095927.htm>.

5. C.-H.C. Cheng, P.A. Cziko, and C.W. Evans, "Non-Hepatic Origin of Notothenoid Antifreeze Reveals Pancreatic Synthesis as Common Mechanism in Polar Fish Avoidance."

Proceedings of the National Academy of Sciences U.S.A., 103L 10491–10496, 2006.

6. Diana Yates, "Study: Antifreeze Proteins in Antarctic Fishes Prevent Freezing…and Melting," News Bureau, University of Illinois, accessed February 1, 2014, <http://news.illinois.edu/news/14/0922ice_fish_cheng.html>.

7. Bureau of Labor Statistics, US Department of Labor, *Occupational Outlook Handbook, 2014–15 Edition*, Zoologists and Wildlife Biologists, <http://www.bls.gov/oes/current/oes191023.htm>.

Chapter 8. Climate Clues to Ice Melt

1. Personal interview, Eugene Domack, February 20, 2007. Unless otherwise indicated, all quotes from Domack come from this interview.

2. Eugene Domack et. al., "Stability of the Larsen B Ice Shelf on the Antarctic Peninsula During the Holocene Epoch," *Nature* 436, August 4, 2005, 681–685.

3. M. Rebesco et. al., "Boundary Condition of Grounding Lines Prior to Collapse, Larsen-B Ice Shelf, Antarctica," *Science* 345, No. 6202, September 12, 2014, 1354–1358.

4. E. Rignot et. al., "Widespread, Rapid Grounding Line Retreat of Pine Island, Thwaites, Smith, and Kohler Glaciers, West Antarctica, from 1992 to 2011," *Geophysical Research Letters* 41, Issue 10, May 28, 2014, 3502–3509.

5. Andrea Baer, "Antarctic Current Circles the World," *The Antarctic Sun*, December 15, 2002, 1, 11, <http://antarcticsun.usap.gov/>.

6. Gabriele C. Hegerl and Francis W. Zwiers, "Understanding and Attributing Climate Change," *Intergovernmental Panel on Climate Change. Working Group I: The Physical Basis of*

Climate Change (2007), <http://ipcc-wg1.ucar.edu/wg1/wg1-report.html>.

7. Melissa Hendricks, "Antarctica Called Him," *Hamilton Alumni Review Online*, Fall 2005, <http://www.hamilton.edu/magazine/2005/fall/antarctica.html>.

8. Eugene Domack, "Antarctica 2006: Journals—Week 1, Friday, April 14," accessed February 13, 2015, <http://www.hamilton.edu/news/exp/Antarctica/2006/week1.html>.

9. Bureau of Labor Statistics, US Department of Labor, *Occupational Outlook Handbook, 2014–15 Edition*, Geoscientists, <http://www.bls.gov/oes/current/oes192042.htm>.

10. Eugene Domack, "Antarctica 2006: Journals—Week 3, Friday, April 28," accessed February 13, 2015, <http://www.hamilton.edu/news/exp/Antarctica/2006/week3.html>.

11. Luis Andres Henao and Seth Borenstein, "'Ground Zero of Climate Change': Antarctic's Melting Ice Could Reshape Continents," *Associated Press*, San Jose Mercury News, February 27, 2015, <http://www.mercurynews.com/science/ci_27611420/ground-zero-climate-change-antarctics-melting-ice-could>.

Glossary

asteroid—A small rocky body orbiting the sun.

comet—An object in outer space consisting of ice and dust. When a comet is near the sun, it has a tail of gas and dust particles pointing away from the sun.

electromagnetic radiation—A kind of radiation, or energy, including visible light, radio waves, gamma rays, X-rays, and microwaves.

glacier—A slowly moving mass or river of ice formed by the accumulation and compaction of snow.

Global Positioning System (GPS)—A method that uses information from satellites orbiting Earth to let users know their exact longitude and latitude.

gravitational waves—Ripples in space time.

ice sheet—A permanent layer of ice covering a large tract of land, especially a polar region.

ice shelf—A sheet of ice floating on an ocean, and attached to a landmass.

Jurassic—The time between the Triassic and Cretaceous periods. It lasted from about 208 million to 146 million years ago.

meteor—A body of matter from outer space that enters Earth's atmosphere, appearing as a streak of light.

meteorite—A meteor that survives its passage through Earth's atmosphere and reaches the ground.

microbe—A tiny form of life that can only be seen with the help of a microscope. Examples include bacteria, some fungi and many parasites.

mitochondria—Structures inside the cell responsible for producing energy.

nematode—A type of worm with a slender, round body. Nematodes are found in soil and water. Many are parasites.

niche—A habitat that contains the things necessary for a particular plant or animal to live.

ozone—A gas formed when oxygen reacts with electrical discharges or ultraviolet light.

parasite—An organism that lives in or on another organism (its host). It gets nutrition from the host, at the host's expense.

plate tectonics—A theory explaining the evidence for large-scale movements of Earth's crust.

radiocarbon dating—The determination of the age of an object from the amounts of different types of carbon it contains.

sublimate—To change from a solid directly into a gas, without becoming a liquid first.

Triassic—The time before the Jurassic period. The Triassic period lasted from about 248 million to 208 million years ago.

Further Reading

Books

Johnson, Kristin. *Endurance Expedition*. Edina, Minn.: ABDO, 2011

Kramme, Michael. *Exploring Antarctica*. Greensboro, N.C.: Mark Twain Media, 2012.

Shuckburgh, Emily, and Catherine Chambers. *Polar Scientist: The Coolest Job on the Planet*. Chicago: Raintree, 2014.

Walker, Gabrielle. *Antarctica: An Intimate Portrait of a Mysterious Continent*. New York: Houghton Mifflin Harcourt, 2013.

White, Andrea. *Surviving Antarctica*. New York, HarperCollins, 2011. Kindle edition.

Video

Antarctica: A Year on Ice. DVD. Directed by Anthony Powell. Chicago: Music Box Films, 2015. 98 min.

Experience the people, the science, and the nature of Antarctica over a one-year time span.

Web Sites

antarcticaonline.com/home/home.htm

Includes photos, history, links to researchers, and descriptions of life in Antarctica.

usap.gov

Provides the latest updates about American research being done in Antarctica.

antarcticsun.usap.gov

The Antarctic Sun includes news about Antarctica's scientists, programs, and geography.

Index